School Day Skills

Grade 1

Say the name of the first picture in the row. Circle pictures whose names begin with the same sound.

Winter • Week 2, Day 1

chair

shell

Roll dice to find two addends. Write them on the first two lines. Then, **add** to find the sum.

1. _____ + _____ = _____

2. _____ + _____ = _____

3. _____ + _____ = _____

4. _____ + _____ = _____

School Day Skills • Grade 1

105

274

Thinking Kids®
An imprint of Carson-Dellosa Publishing LLC
P.O. Box 35665
Greensboro, NC 27425 USA

Thinking Kids®
Carson-Dellosa Publishing LLC
P.O. Box 35665
Greensboro, NC 27425 USA

ISBN 978-1-4838-3113-8

Table of Contents

Practice writing the letters.

Aa

Bb

Cc

Dd

Write the **short a** word that names each picture.

cap pan mat van bat jam

Count the number in each group. Draw a line to the correct number.

1
2
3
4
5
6
7
8
9
10

Say each picture name. If the name has the **short e** sound, color the space yellow.

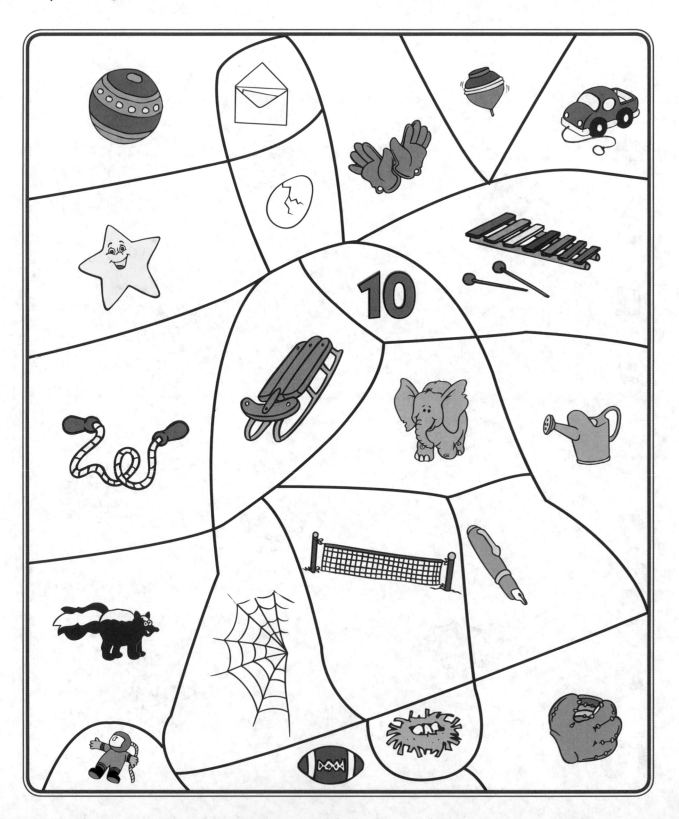

Count to 20. Write the missing numbers.

1				
6				
11			14	
			19	

Practice writing the letters.

Count by **fives**. Circle the numbers you use. On the lines, write the numbers you circled.

1	2	3	4	5	6	7	8	9	10
11	12	13	14	15	16	17	18	19	20
21	22	23	24	25	26	27	28	29	30
31	32	33	34	35	36	37	38	39	40
41	42	43	44	45	46	47	48	49	50

_____ _____ _____ _____ _____

_____ _____ _____ _____ _____

Practice writing the letters.

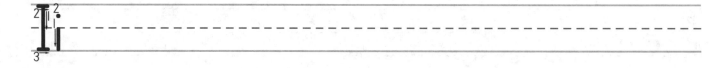

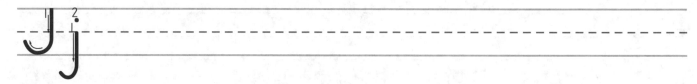

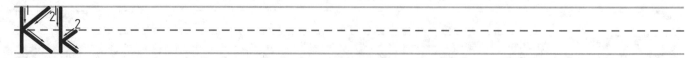

Add.

6 + 2 = _____

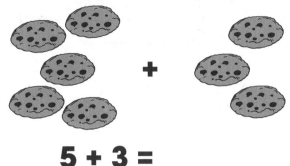

5 + 3 = _____

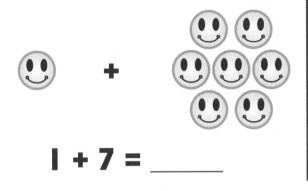

1 + 7 = _____

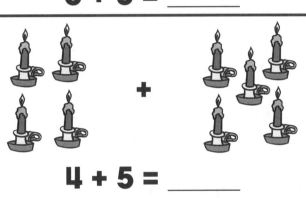

4 + 5 = _____

Write **i** on each line. Color the picture that matches the word.

l _ d

s _ x

m _ lk

g _ ft

Write a **short o** word to complete each sentence.

got	mom	on	hot

1. Put it _____ top of the box.

2. Will his _____ let us play?

3. Bob _____ a rock in his sock.

4. That pot is very _____.

Draw what comes next in each pattern.

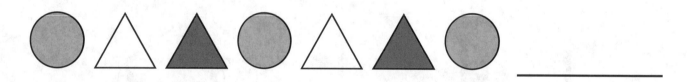

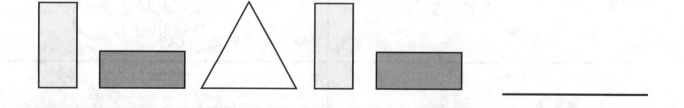

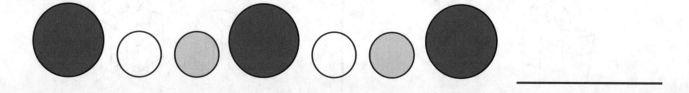

Write numbers to complete the addition problems. Draw the missing pictures.

 + 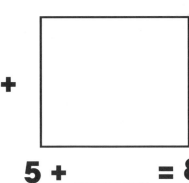 =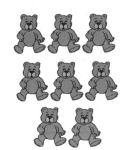

5 + _____ = 8

 +  =

3 + _____ = 6

Practice writing the letters.

Practice writing the letters.

Say each picture name. Circle the letter that matches its **beginning** sound. Color the pictures.

b   t   c

t   c   s

t   c   s

b   t   c

b   c   s

t   c   s

Add or **subtract** to solve the problems. Use the code to color the fruit.

3 = yellow	5 = orange	7 = yellow	9 = red
4 = red	6 = purple	8 = green	10 = brown

$\begin{array}{r} 9 \\ -\ 4 \\ \hline \end{array}$

$\begin{array}{r} 7 \\ +\ 3 \\ \hline \end{array}$

$\begin{array}{r} 6 \\ -\ 3 \\ \hline \end{array}$

$\begin{array}{r} 1 \\ +\ 3 \\ \hline \end{array}$

$\begin{array}{r} 9 \\ -\ 2 \\ \hline \end{array}$

$\begin{array}{r} 7 \\ +\ 2 \\ \hline \end{array}$

$\begin{array}{r} 10 \\ -\ 2 \\ \hline \end{array}$

$\begin{array}{r} 6 \\ +\ 3 \\ \hline \end{array}$

$\begin{array}{r} 8 \\ -\ 2 \\ \hline \end{array}$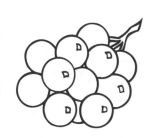

Say each picture name. If the name has the **short u** sound, color the space yellow.

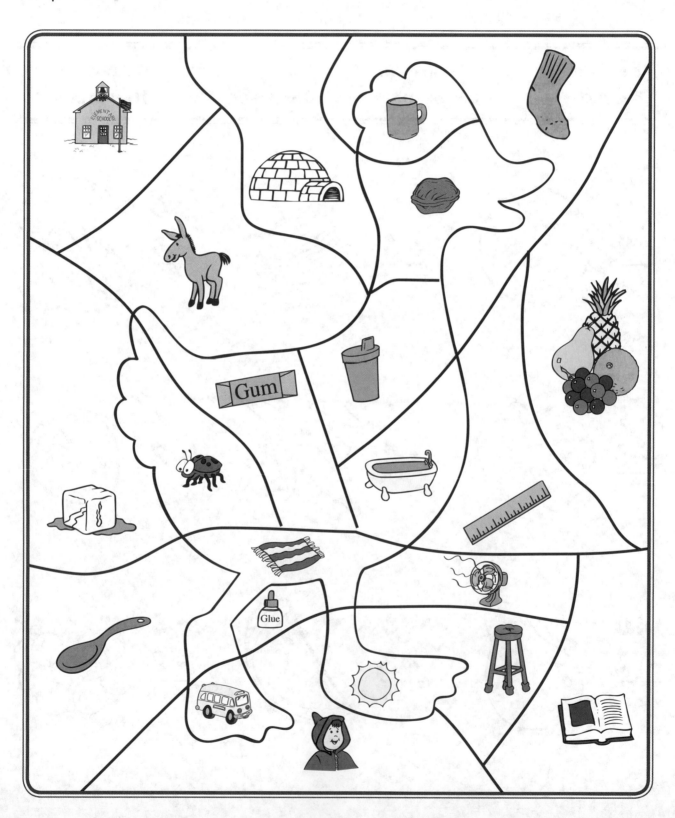

Subtract.

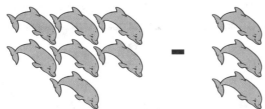

How many s are left?

7 - 3 = _____

How many s are left?

6 - 5 = _____

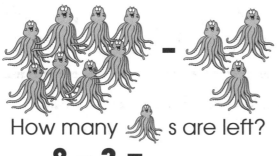

How many s are left?

8 - 3 = _____

How many s are left?

5 - 2 = _____

Practice writing the letters.

Circle the picture that matches the addition problem.

2 + 4 = 6

3 + 3 = 6

3 + 4 = 7

1 + 6 = 7

Practice writing the letters.

Count each group of tally marks. Write the number on the line.
Each mark stands for one: I. Five tally marks look like this: 卌.

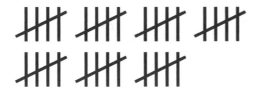 _____

 _____

 _____

_____

Say each picture name. Circle the letter that matches its **beginning** sound. Color the pictures.

 l q z

 l y z

 q y z

 l y z

 l y z

 q y z

Add or **subtract** to solve the problems. Match your answers to the code to color the quilt.

6 = blue   8 = green   10 = orange

7 = yellow   9 = red

Match the **lowercase** letter to the **uppercase** letter.

a	C
f	H
c	J
h	E
e	A
j	F
g	D
b	B
i	M
d	G
k	I
l	L
m	K

Match the **lowercase** letter to the **uppercase** letter.

n	U
s	P
p	R
u	Q
r	N
q	S
t	V
y	O
v	T
o	W
x	Z
w	Y
z	X

Trace the **circles** in **red**. Trace the **squares** in **blue**. Trace the **rectangles** in yellow. Trace the **triangles** in green. Trace the **ovals** in **purple**. Trace the **rhombuses** in orange.

Count by **tens**. Circle the numbers you use. On the lines, write the numbers you circled.

1	2	3	4	5	6	7	8	9	10
11	12	13	14	15	16	17	18	19	20
21	22	23	24	25	26	27	28	29	30
31	32	33	34	35	36	37	38	39	40
41	42	43	44	45	46	47	48	49	50

_____ _____ _____ _____ _____

Count the sheep on each hill. Write the number on the tree.

Say the name of each picture. Then, write the letter that makes its **beginning** sound.

____acket

____oat

____og

____itt

____ipper

____ock

____icket

____an

Nouns can name people. Read the nouns. On each line, write a noun that names a person.

store	child	baby	teacher
table	park	woman	sock

person

_____   _____

_____   _____

Count by **tens** to draw the path the boy takes to the store.

A **pronoun** can take the place of a noun in a sentence. Circle the pronoun that can take the place of the **bold** word.

1. **My mother** is a pilot.   a. They   b. She

2. **My brother and I** have flown   a. We   b. They
   with her.

3. **My brother** wants to be a pilot, too.   a. It   b. He

Write a **short a** word to name each picture. Then, read the rhyming words on each train.

Write a **long a** word to name each picture. **Hint:** Each word ends with **silent e** as in **lake**. Read the rhyming words on each train.

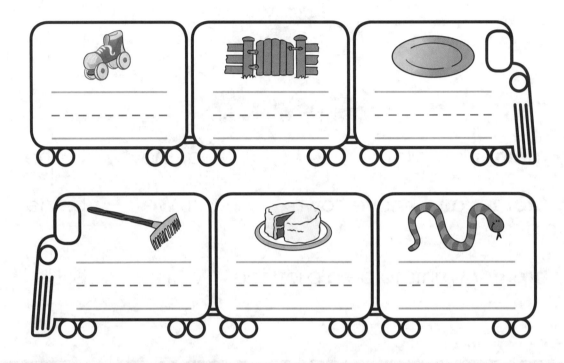

Nouns can name places. Read the nouns. On each line, write a noun that names a place.

| store | zoo | teacher | table |
| park | gym | woman | sock |

place

Add to fill in the chart. Write the sums where the columns and rows meet. The first one is done for you.

+	1	2	3	4	5	6	7	8	9
1	2								
2									
3									
4									
5									
6									
7									
8									
9									

Count each group of **tens**. Write a number on the line.

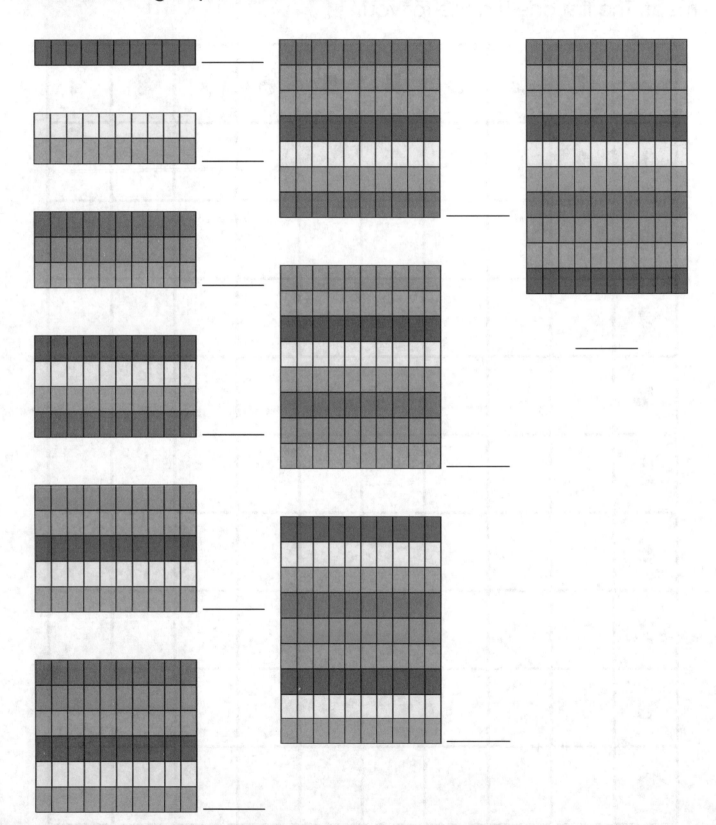

Say the name of each picture. If it has the **short a** sound, color it **red**. If it has the **long a** sound, color it yellow.

ă ā

Short e is the sound you hear in **hen**. **Long e** is the sound you hear in **bee**. Say the name of each picture. If you hear **short e**, draw a line to the hen. If you hear **long e**, draw a line to the bee.

hen

bee

Write addition problems in two different ways for each picture story. The first one is done for you.

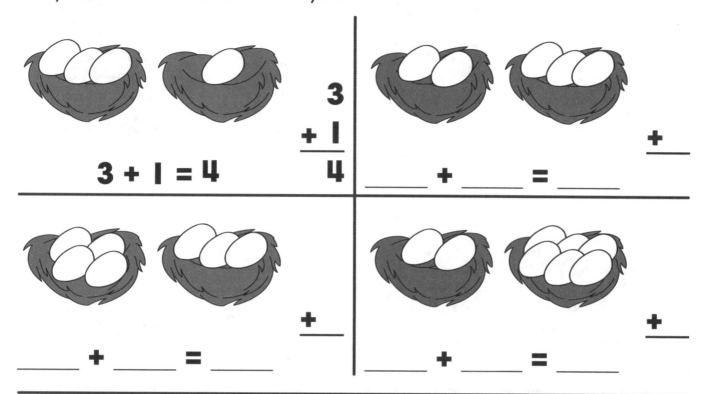

3 + 1 = 4

3
+ 1
___
4

_____ + _____ = _____

+
___

_____ + _____ = _____

+
___

_____ + _____ = _____

+
___

Count the objects. Write a number on each line to complete the addition problem. Then, switch the addends and write another addition problem with the same sum. The first one is done for you.

If ___3___ + ___8___ = __11__ , so does ___8___ + ___3___ .

If _____ + _____ = _____ , so does _____ + _____ .

Circle the pictures whose names have the **short e** sound. Draw a triangle around the pictures whose names have the **long e** sound.

  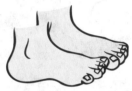

Nouns can name things. Read the nouns. On each line, write a noun that names a thing.

store	baby	teacher	table
cat	park	sock	horse

thing

_____ _____

- - - - - - - - - - - - - - - - - - - - - - - - - -

_____ _____

- - - - - - - - - - - - - - - - - - - - - - - - - -

Subtract. Circle the picture that matches the subtraction problem.

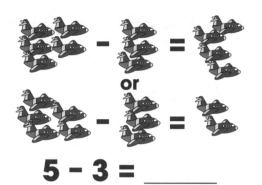

5 - 3 = _____

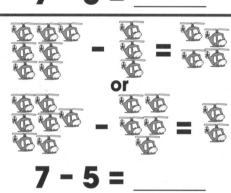

7 - 3 = _____

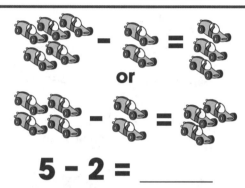

5 - 2 = _____

7 - 5 = _____

How long do you think each activity takes? Circle the best estimate.

I minute   I hour

I minute   I hour

I minute   I hour

I minute   I hour

Add.

1 + 7 = _____

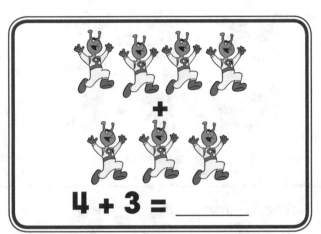

4 + 3 = _____

3 + 3 = _____

4 + 5 = _____

A **pronoun** can take the place of a noun in a sentence. Circle the pronoun that can take the place of the **bold** word.

1. **Mother** says flying is fun.   a. She   b. He

2. **Dad** loves to fly.   a. They   b. He

3. **My brother** is older than I am.   a. He   b. We

4. **The backpack** is under the table.   a. She   b. It

Say the name of each picture. Then, write the letter that makes its **beginning** sound.

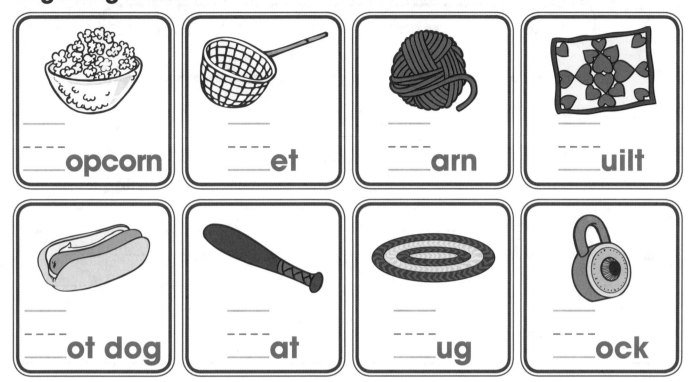

_____
___opcorn

_____
___et

_____
___arn

_____
___uilt

_____
___ot dog

_____
___at

_____
___ug

_____
___ock

Draw and color the missing shape in each pattern.

Write each **noun** in the correct column.

| shoe | school | friend | robot |
| | boy | theater | |

person

place

thing

Say each picture name. Write the letter that makes its **beginning** sound. Color the pictures.

How many things are in the picture? Count each type of object.
Write the numbers in the boxes.

Look at the shapes. Answer the questions.

1. How many all-white shapes? _____

2. How many all-blue shapes? _____

3. How many half-white shapes? _____

4. How many all-blue stars? _____

5. How many all-white circles? _____

6. How many half-blue shapes? _____

Write a **short i** word to complete each sentence.

sit	dig	hit	lid

1. The dog can _____ a hole.

2. Put the _____ on the pan.

3. He will _____ on the bench.

4. Tom _____ the ball into the stands.

Write **pronouns** to take the place of the underlined words.

1. <u>A big ball</u> was held at the palace.

_____

2. <u>Cinderella</u> was left at home to work.

_____

3. <u>A fairy godmother</u> came to help her go to the ball.

_____

4. <u>The prince and Cinderella</u> were married.

_____

You hear **short i** in **pig**. You hear **long i** in **kite**. Circle words with the **short i** sound. Draw an X on words with the **long i** sound.

pin

five

pig

slide

kite

lid

tie

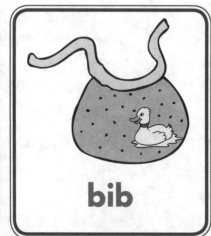

bib

pie

Draw what comes next in each pattern.

 _____

 _____

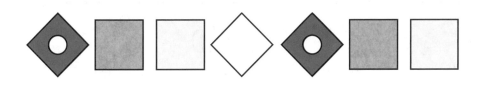 _____

Count the objects. Write a number on each line to complete the addition problem. Then, switch the addends and write another addition problem with the same sum.

If _____ + _____ = _____ , so does _____ + _____ .

If _____ + _____ = _____ , so does _____ + _____ .

Say each letter sound. Color the pictures in each row that begin with that sound.

A **verb** names an action. A **present-tense verb** tells what is happening now. Write a present-tense verb to complete each sentence.

| mows | pick | rakes |

1. The kids _____.

2. Dave _____.

3. Mara _____.

Write **+** or **–** in each problem to show if you should **add** or **subtract**. Solve the problems.

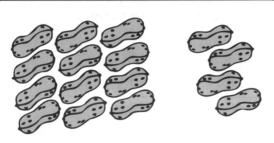

How many s are left?

12   4 = _____

How many s in all?

6   8 = _____

How many s are left?

4   4 = _____

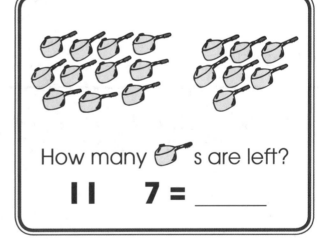

How many s are left?

11   7 = _____

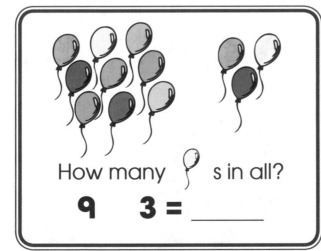

How many s in all?

9   3 = _____

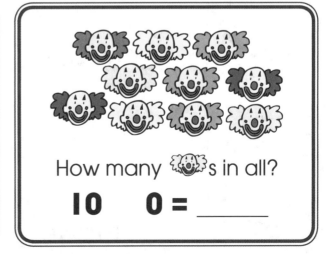

How many s in all?

10   0 = _____

Write a **short o** word to complete each sentence.

| lot | hop | mop | not |

1. A rabbit will _____ on top of the log.

2. We had a _____ of fun at the pond.

3. Rob will _____ up the spilled milk.

4. Rhonda did _____ stop at the shop.

When the long hand is on 12, the short hand shows the **hour**. Write the time shown on each clock.

_____ o'clock

_____ o'clock

_____ o'clock

_____ o'clock

Write a **present-tense verb** under each picture to tell what is happening now.

cheers	chases	hits	throws

Draw shapes to continue the patterns.

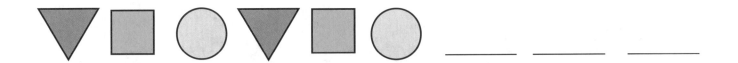

Add. Write each sum on a flowerpot.

4 + 6 =

1 + 9 =

7 + 1 =

7 + 3 =

5 + 2 =

6 + 1 =

Fill in the circles below the **nouns**.

1. Use a shovel to dig.
   ○   ○

2. We will make a garden.
   ○   ○

3. Our friends can help.
   ○   ○

4. Drop one in each hole.
   ○   ○

5. The seeds will grow.
   ○   ○

Name_____

Say the name of each picture. If you hear the **short o** sound, write **S** on the line. If you hear the **long o** sound, write **L** on the line.

_ _ _ _ _ _

_ _ _ _ _ _

_ _ _ _ _ _

_ _ _ _ _ _

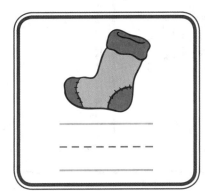
_ _ _ _ _ _

_ _ _ _ _ _

Write numbers to continue the patterns.

1   5   2   5   1   5   2   ___   ___   ___

5   4   6   5   4   6   5   ___   ___   ___

9   9   8   9   9   9   8   9   ___   ___   ___

Say the name of each picture. Write the letter that makes the **beginning** sound.

____at

____oat

____ite

____am

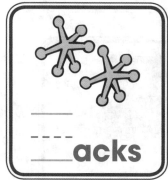

____acks

____ate

____ey

____appy

Count each group and write the number on the line. Then, **add** and write the sum.

_____ balloons

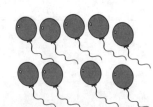

_____ balloons

How many in all? _____

_____ flowers

_____ flowers

How many in all? _____

Write each **noun** in the correct column.

| knee | girl | baby | game | uncle |
| library | song | restaurant | bedroom | |

person	place	thing

Write the time shown on each clock.

_____ o'clock   _____ o'clock   _____ o'clock

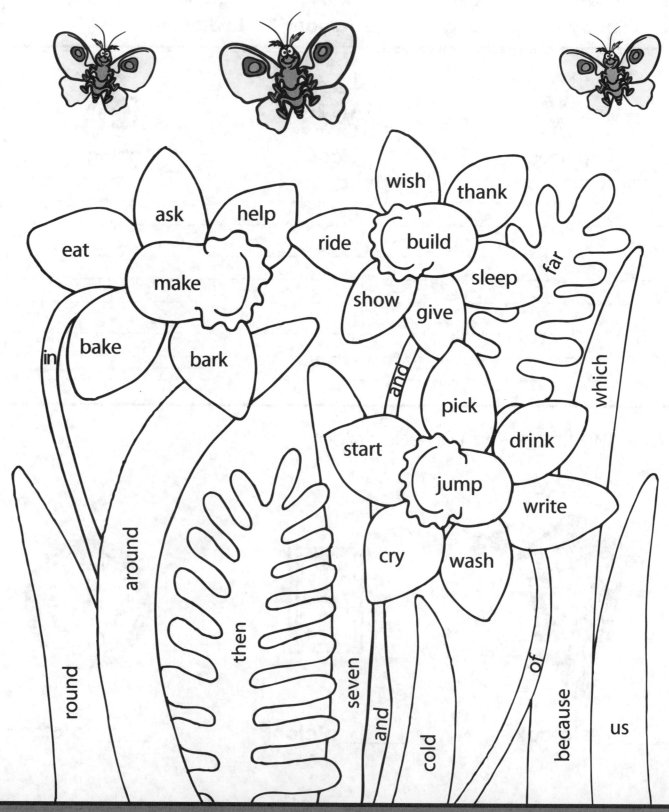

A **verb** tells what a person, animal, or thing does. Color the spaces with verbs yellow. Color the other spaces **green**.

You hear the **short u** sound in **bug**. You hear the **long u** sound in **blue**. Circle words with the **short u** sound. Draw a X on words with the **long u** sound.

music

gum

bug

rug

glue

suit

Write the missing numbers.

5 + 4 = 9   3 + 1 = 4   2 + 6 = 8

4 + ___ = 9   1 + ___ = 4   6 + ___ = 8

---

6 + 1 = 7   4 + 3 = 7   1 + 9 = 10

1 + ___ = 7   3 + ___ = 7   9 + ___ = 10

Say the name of each picture. If you hear the **short u** sound, write **u** in the umbrella column. If you hear the **long u** sound, write **u** in the unicorn column.

Ū

Ŭ

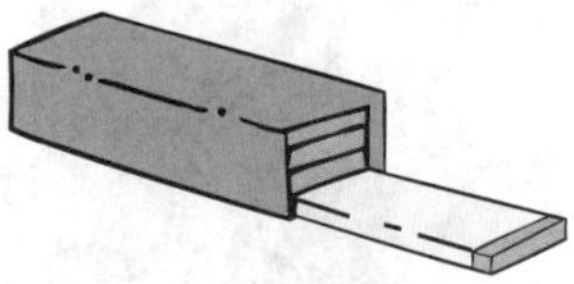

Color the **second** ball **brown**.

Color the **sixth** ball yellow.

Color the **fifth** ball **green**.

Subtract.

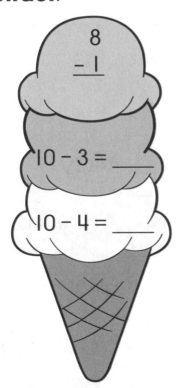

8
−1

10 − 3 = ____

10 − 4 = ____

8
−2

10 − 4 = ____

7 − 2 = ____

9
−4

10 − 1 = ____

9 − 1 = ____

A **adjective** describes a person, place, or thing. Write an adjective to describe each picture.

| wet | round | sad | tall |

Write **1** to **12** in the boxes to put the months in order. The first one is done for you.

☐ April   ☐ February   ☐ May

☐ October   ☐ July   ☐ August

☐ December   **1** January   ☐ March

☐ September   ☐ June   ☐ November

Write the number of **ones** blocks. Then, write the sum.

1.  + ▮ = 1 ten + _____ one = _____

2. + ▮▮▮ = 1 ten + _____ ones = _____

3. + ▮▮▮▮▮ = 1 ten + _____ ones = _____
   ▮

Say each picture name. Write the letter that makes the **beginning** sound. Color the pictures.

_____
_ _ _ _ _ _
_____

_____
_ _ _ _ _ _
_____

Write the number of **ones** blocks. Then, write the sum.

1. ⟦⟧⟦⟧⟦⟧⟦⟧⟦⟧ + ▮▮▮▮ = 1 ten + _____ ones = _____

2. ⟦⟧⟦⟧⟦⟧⟦⟧⟦⟧ + ▮▮▮▮▮ ▮▮ = 1 ten + _____ ones = _____

3. ⟦⟧⟦⟧⟦⟧⟦⟧⟦⟧ ⟦⟧⟦⟧⟦⟧⟦⟧⟦⟧ + = 2 tens + _____ ones = _____

Write **a**, **e**, **i**, or **u** to complete each short vowel word.

p___n   b___g

p___n   b___g

p___n   b___g

A **adjective** describes a person, place, or thing. Write an adjective to describe each picture.

| sick | cold | long | soft |

_____

- - - - - - - - - - - - - - -

_____

_____

- - - - - - - - - - - - - - -

_____

_____

- - - - - - - - - - - - - - -

_____

_____

- - - - - - - - - - - - - - -

_____

Write the missing numbers.

3, _____ , 5   7, _____ , 9   8, _____ , 10

13, _____ , 15   _____ , 20, 21   _____ , 29, 30

39, 40, _____   _____ , 44, 45   _____ , 50, 51

Write the correct **pronoun** in each blank.

He　　　She　　　It

1. Sarah had a birthday party.

   _____

   - - - - - - - - - -
   _____ invited six friends.

2. The kitten likes to play.

   _____

   - - - - - - - - - -
   _____ likes to tug on shoelaces.

3. Ed is seven years old.

   _____

   - - - - - - - - - -
   _____ is in the second grade.

Write the missing numbers in the problems.

$5 + \bigcirc = 14$　　$12 + \bigcirc = 18$　　$7 + \bigcirc = 13$

$4 + \bigcirc = 17$　　$9 + \bigcirc = 15$　　$6 + \bigcirc = 16$

$11 + \bigcirc = 16$　　$8 + \bigcirc = 13$

You hear **long a** in **lake**. You hear **long e** in **bee**. You hear **long i** in **ride**. Color the pictures that have the **long vowel sound** shown at the beginning of the row.

Color the boxes to show how many spots are on each turtle shell.

Write the letter that makes the **beginning** sound for each small picture. Then, color the big picture.

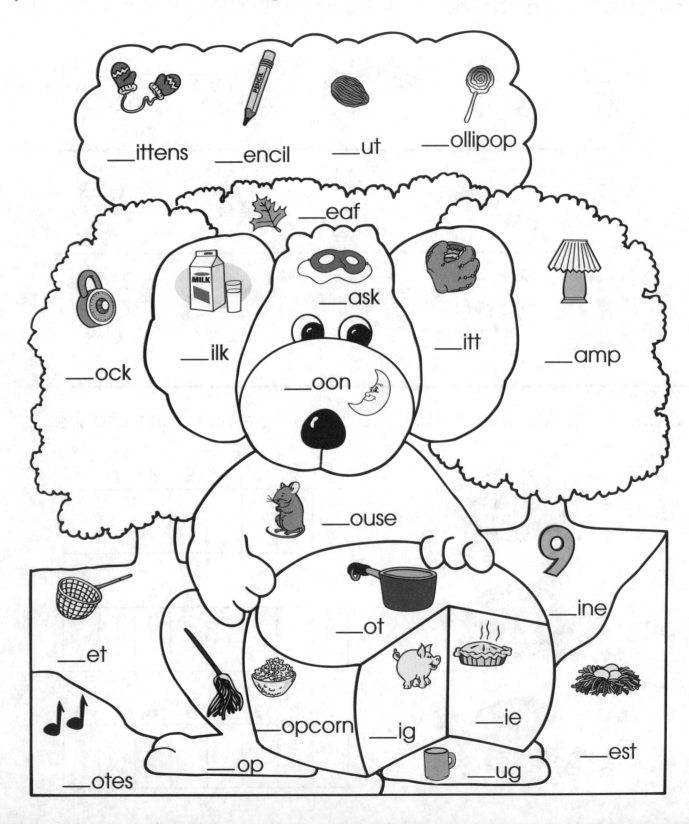

__ittens   __encil   __ut   __ollipop

__eaf

__ock   __ilk   __ask   __itt   __amp

__oon

__ouse

__et   __ot   __ine

__otes   __opcorn   __ig   __ie   __ug   __est

Count the crayons in each box. Write the number on the line. Then, **subtract** to solve the problems. Circle the problems that have the same answer as the number of crayons in the box.

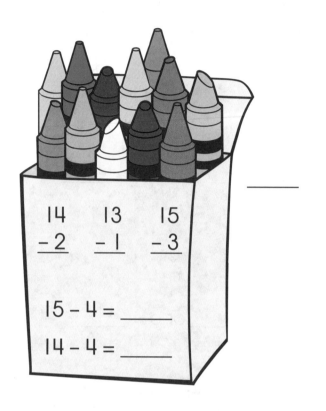

_____

$$\begin{array}{ccc} 14 & 13 & 15 \\ -2 & -1 & -3 \end{array}$$

$15 - 4 =$ _____

$14 - 4 =$ _____

_____

$$\begin{array}{cc} 15 & 12 \\ -1 & -1 \end{array}$$

$13 - 1 =$ _____

$15 - 1 =$ _____

$12 - 2 =$ _____

Write the missing numbers.

_____ , 54, 55   _____ , 60, 61   62, _____ , 64

69, 70, _____   74, 75, _____   77, 78, _____

88, _____ , 90   _____ , 85, 86   80, _____ , 82

For each problem, write the number of **tens** and **ones** blocks.
Then, write the sum.

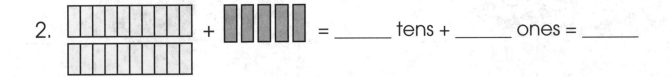

1. [tens block] + [ones blocks] = _____ ten + _____ ones = _____

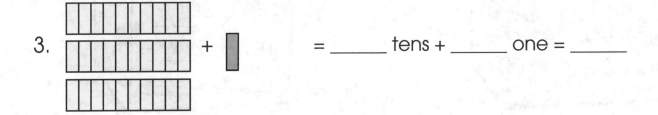

2. [tens blocks] + [ones blocks] = _____ tens + _____ ones = _____

3. [tens blocks] + [one block] = _____ tens + _____ one = _____

You hear **long o** in **boat**. You hear **long u** in **cute**. Color the
pictures that have the **long vowel sound** shown at the beginning
of the row.

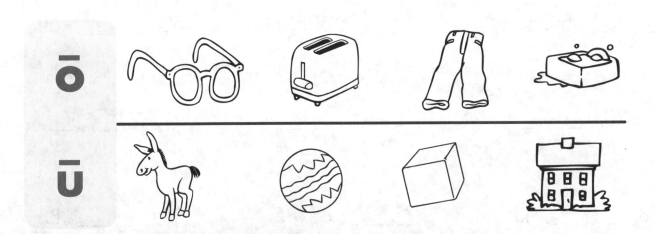

Circle the **noun** in each sentence.

The balloon soared high.

The world below looked small.

Clouds were all around.

I felt like a bird.

Write the missing numbers in the problems.

9 + ☐ = 17   ☐ + 10 = 14   ☐ + 1 = 12

☐ + 3 = 12   ☐ + 2 = 14   ☐ + 8 = 15

☐ + 7 = 10   ☐ + 9 = 18   ☐ + 6 = 11

Count the crayons in each box. Write the number on the line. Then, **subtract** to solve the problems. Circle the problems that have the same answer as the number of crayons in the box.

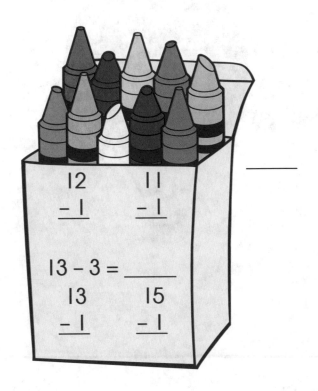

$$12 \atop -\ 1$$ $$11 \atop -\ 1$$ _____

$$13 - 3 = $$ _____

$$13 \atop -\ 1$$ $$15 \atop -\ 1$$

$$15 - 2 = $$ _____   _____

$$14 \atop -\ 2$$ $$14 \atop -\ 0$$

$$14 - 1 = $$ _____

$$15 - 3 = $$ _____

Write **a**, **i**, **o**, or **u** to complete each short vowel word.

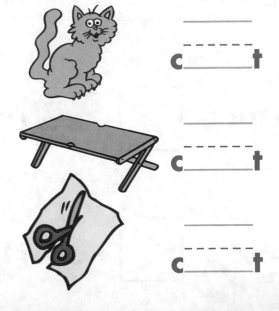

c___t

c___t

c___t

h___t

h___t

h___t

Draw lines to match clocks that show the same time.

2:00

3:00

9:00

A **verb** names an action. A **present-tense verb** tells what is happening now. Write a present-tense verb to complete each sentence.

| weeds | plants | waters |

1. Troy _____.

2. Mother _____.

3. Jess _____.

When you add **super silent e** to the end of some words, the **short vowel sound** changes to a **long vowel sound**. Say the word under the first picture. Write the same word under the second picture, but add **super silent e** to the end of the word. Read the long vowel words you wrote.

pet

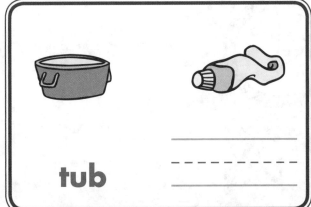

tub

man

kit

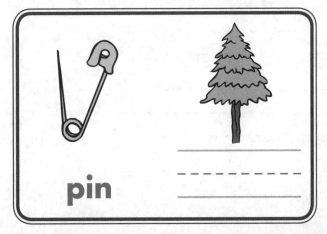

pin

cap

Write each problem on the life jacket with the correct answer.

11 + 6	7 + 8	8 + 8
6 + 9	8 + 9	9 + 7
7 + 9	8 + 7	9 + 8

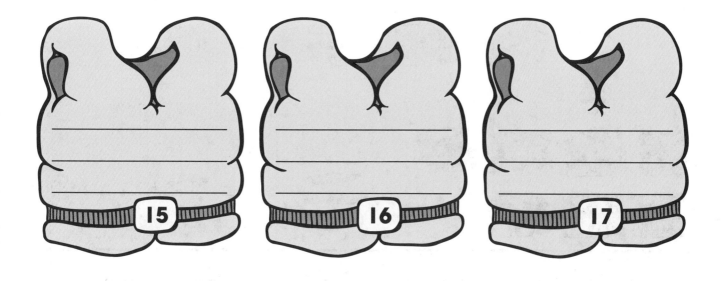

15   16   17

Write the missing numbers.

90, 91, _____   110, 111,_____   104, _____ , 106

99, 100, _____   _____ , 101, 102   _____ , 119, 120

12, 13, _____   86, _____ , 88   _____ , 51, 52

Count the groups of ten crayons and write the number of **tens**.
Count the other crayons and write the number of **ones**.

+ = _____ ten + _____ one

+ = _____ tens + _____ ones

+ = _____ tens + _____ ones

Circle the **adjective** in each sentence. Draw a line from the
sentence to the matching picture.

1. The hungry dog is eating.

2. The tiny bird is flying.

3. Horses have long legs.

Write **a**, **e**, **i**, **o**, or **u** in each blank to complete the words with a **long vowel sound**.

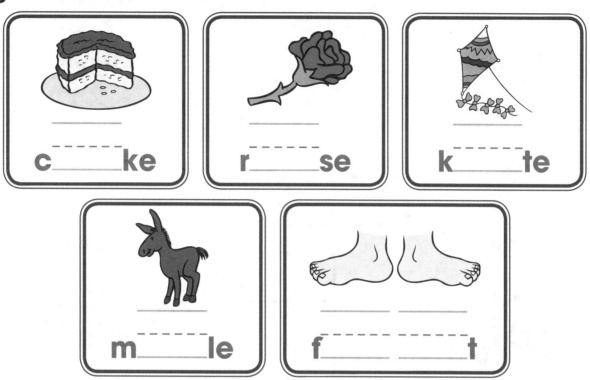

c___ke   r___se   k___te

m___le   f___t

Color the shapes that have four sides.

Say each picture name. Write the missing vowel **a**, **e**, **i**, **o**, or **u** in the puzzle.

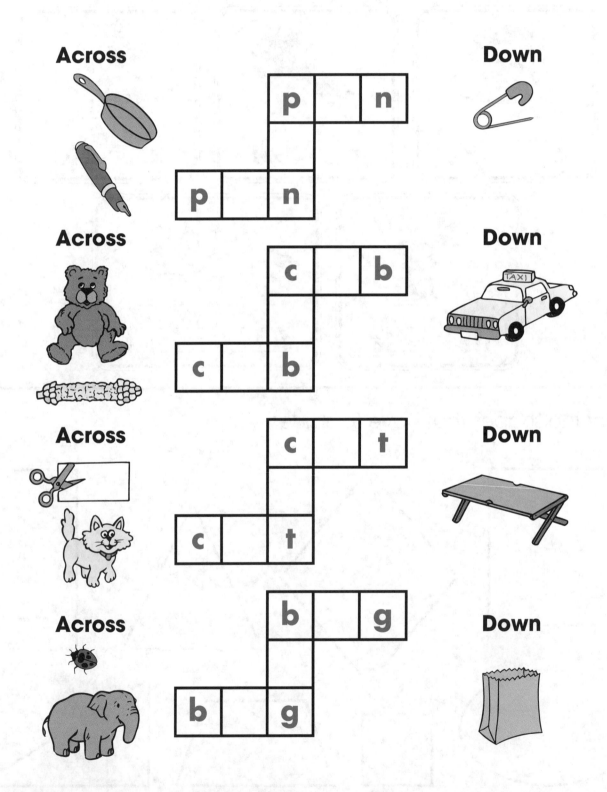

Across

Down

Across

Down

Across

Down

Across

Down

Write the missing numbers.

20				
	26			
30				**34**
		37		

Color the shapes that have no corners.

Color words and number words are **adjectives**. Underline the describing word in each sentence. Draw a picture for each sentence.

A yellow moon was in the sky.

Two worms are on the road.

Say each picture name. Write the letter that makes the **ending** sound.

 fla___

 boo___

 bo___

 we___

 mo___

 ca___

 ga___

 ha___

Write the number of **tens** and **ones** in each number.

35 _____ tens _____ ones

8 _____ tens _____ ones

49 _____ tens _____ ones

Add or **subtract**. If the answer is greater than 12, color the space **brown**. Color the rest **green**.

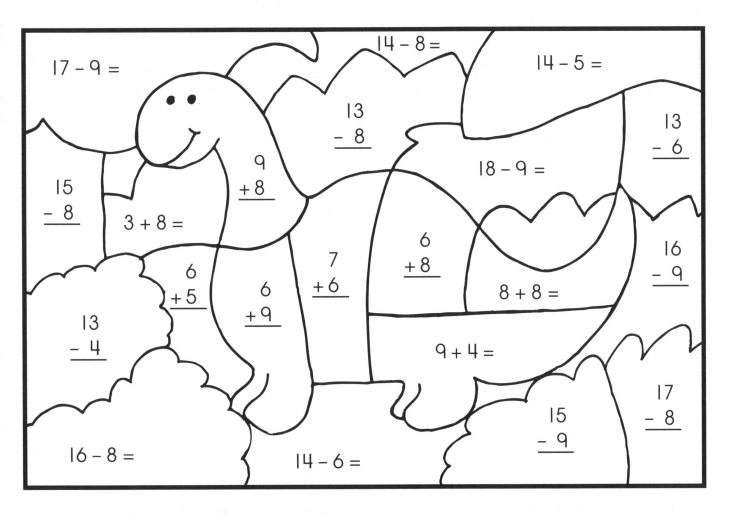

Say each picture name. Write the letter that makes the **ending** sound.

lea____

pi____

be____

duc____

ca____

si____

dru____

roo____

Color the shapes that have three sides.

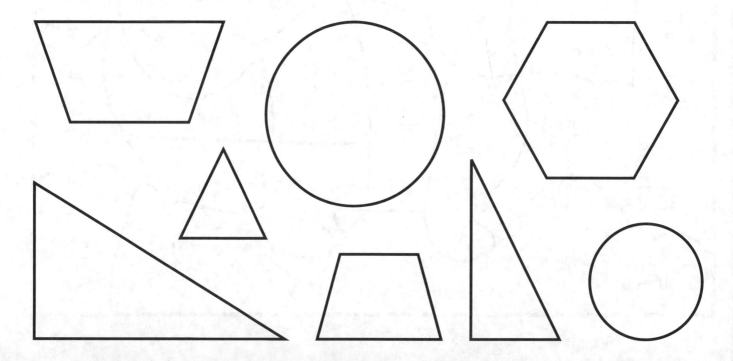

A **preposition** is a word that can tell **where** something is. In a sentence, it shows the relationship between two nouns or pronouns. Some prepositions that tell where are **above**, **around**, **beside**, **in**, **over**, and **under**. In each sentence, look at the underlined nouns. Circle a preposition that tells where.

1. The <u>dog</u> ran fast around the <u>house</u>.

2. I planted <u>flowers</u> in my <u>garden</u>.

3. My <u>kite</u> flew high above the <u>trees</u>.

4. Beside the <u>pond</u>, there was a <u>playground</u>.

_____

Look at the number of **tens** and **ones**. Write a two-digit number to solve each problem.

6 tens + 3 ones = _____   5 tens + 1 one = _____

3 tens + 8 ones = _____   9 tens + 7 ones = _____

4 tens + 5 ones = _____   2 tens + 8 ones = _____

Underline two nouns or pronouns in each sentence. Then, write a **preposition** to complete the sentence.

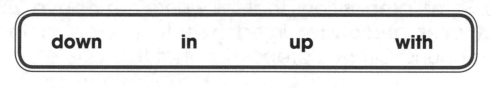

| down | in | up | with |

1. The money is _____ my bank.

2. My cousin came _____ me.

3. The boy climbed _____ the tree.

4. A bike zoomed _____ the hill.

Write the numbers that are:

next in order	one less	one greater
23, ____ , ____	____ , 16	6, ____
74, ____ , ____	____ , 47	25, ____
27, ____ , ____	____ , 50	99, ____
97, ____ , ____	____ , 33	50, ____
29, ____ , ____	____ , 62	33, ____

The **long a** sound can be spelled **ai** or **ay**. Write **long a** words to complete the sentences.

sail	play	mail

1. Can you come outside and _____?

2. The boat has a colorful _____.

3. I will send a card in the _____.

Use the numbers on each train to write fact families.

____ + ____ = ____   ____ + ____ = ____

____ + ____ = ____   ____ + ____ = ____

____ − ____ = ____   ____ − ____ = ____

____ − ____ = ____   ____ − ____ = ____

Fill in the circles below the **verbs**.

1. The dog barks.
   ◯ ◯

2. It pushes the empty bowl on the floor.
   ◯   ◯

3. The dog wants something.
   ◯ ◯

4. The boy feeds his dog.
   ◯ ◯

5. The dog wags its tail.
   ◯ ◯

Add or **subtract**. Draw lines to match the facts. The first one is done for you.

5 + 9 = __14__ •   • 6 + 9 = ____

8 + 7 = ____ •   • 14 – 9 = __5__

15 – 9 = ____ •   • 15 – 7 = ____

17 – 8 = ____ •   • 14 – 7 = ____

7 + 7 = ____ •   • 9 + 8 = ____

Say each picture name. Write the letter that makes its **ending** sound.

pai____

lo____

shel____

cra____

li____

bea____

Write the time shown on each clock.

_____ o'clock

_____ o'clock

_____ o'clock

The **long e** sound can be spelled **ee**, **ea**, or **ey**. Write **ee**, **ea**, or **ey** in the blanks to complete the words.

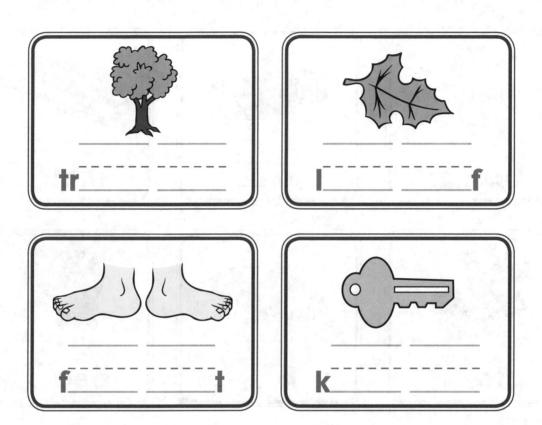

tr_____

l_____ f

f_____ t

k_____

Fill in the missing numbers.

9 + ◯ = 17

17 − ◯ = 8

18 − ◯ = 9

12 − ◯ = 3

8 + ◯ = 14

11 − ◯ = 4

◯ + 5 = 12

16 − ◯ = 9

7 + ◯ = 13

Connect the dots to draw three shapes that have four sides.

A sentence that tells something ends with a **period** (.). Write the **telling sentences**. Begin each one with an uppercase letter. End each one with a period.

this dog is friendly

_____
- -
_____

the bird came to me

_____
- -
_____

Say each picture name. Write the letter that makes its **ending** sound.

mu_____

ha_____

gir_____

broo_____

tu_____

hoo_____

Draw hands on the clock faces to show the time.

9:00

7:00

3:00

Underline two nouns in each sentence. Then, write a **preposition** to complete the sentence.

off	onto	out

1. The baby held _____ the bear.

2. Two kids jumped _____ the dock.

3. The cat peeked _____ of the bag.

Use the numbers on each train to write fact families.

____ + ____ = ____

____ + ____ = ____

____ − ____ = ____

____ − ____ = ____

____ + ____ = ____

____ + ____ = ____

____ − ____ = ____

____ − ____ = ____

Read the first part of each **telling sentence**. Draw a line to the part that completes it. Write a **period (.)** at the end of each sentence.

   1. The truck   carries toys ☐

   2. The train   takes off ☐

   3. The bike   is red ☐

   4. The plane   has wheels ☐

Solve the word problems.

1. Marcus had a package of 20 stickers. He used 11 stickers. How many were left?

_____ stickers

2. 14 kids got to the playground at 12:00. 3 more kids came to the playground at 1:00. How many kids in all were at the playground?

_____ kids

The **long i** sound can be spelled **ie** or **y**. Write **long i** words to complete the sentences.

| pie | why | sky | tie |

1. A plane flies in the _____.

2. _____ is that movie your favorite?

3. Let me _____ my shoe.

4. Would you like a slice of _____?

Color the shapes that have four equal sides.

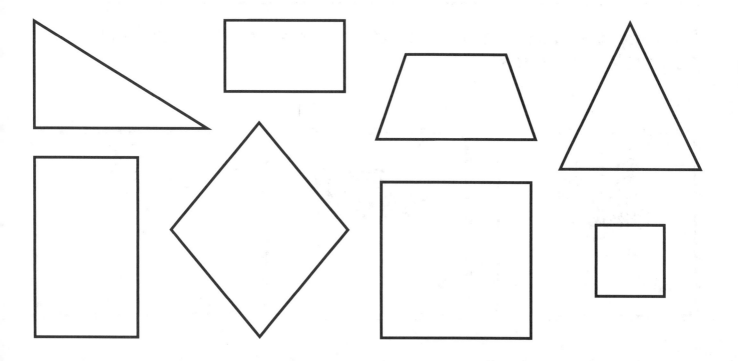

Underline two nouns in each sentence. Then, write a **preposition** to complete the sentence.

by	next	into	from

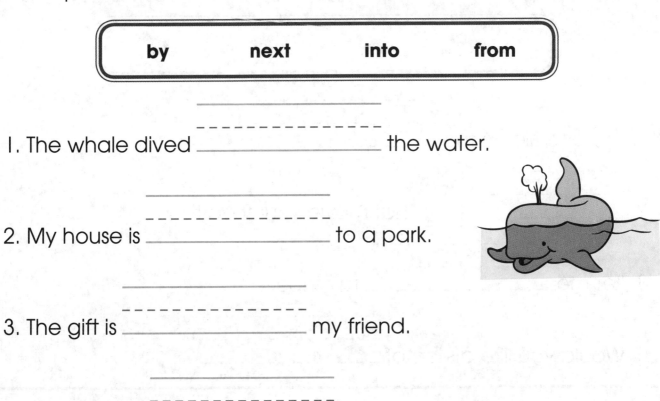

1. The whale dived _____ the water.

2. My house is _____ to a park.

3. The gift is _____ my friend.

4. The library is _____ the post office.

The **long o** sound can be spelled **oa**. Write **oa** in the blanks to complete the words.

c _____ t

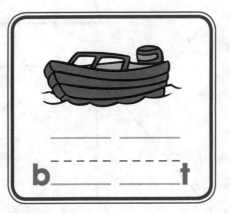

b _____ t

g _____ t

Count to 120. Fill in the missing numbers.

1									
					16				
						27			
	32								
							48		
				55					
								69	
									80
							88		
			94						
101									
			114						

Say the name of each picture. Write a letter that spells its **beginning** sound, **middle** sound, and **ending** sound. Color the pictures.

Count the groups of **ten**. Write the number. There are 0 **ones**, so each number you write will end with 0.

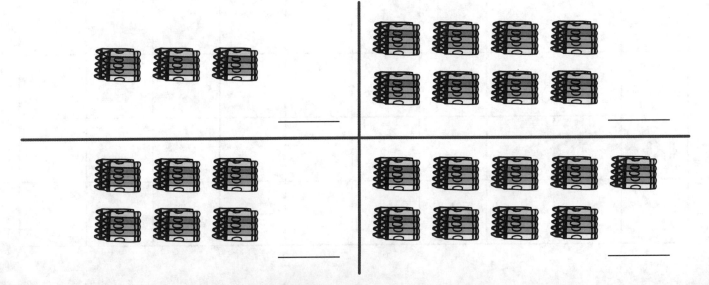

A sentence that asks something ends with a **question mark (?)**. Write the **asking sentences**. Begin each one with an uppercase letter. End each one with a question mark.

do you like to read

_____
- -
_____

what is that book about

_____
- -
_____

Solve the word problems.

1. Kelsey solved 9 clues for a puzzle. There are 18 clues in all. How many more clues does Kelsey have to solve?

   _____ clues

2. Dad made 10 tacos. He made 6 burritos. How many items did he make in all?

   _____ items

The **long u** sound can be spelled **ue** or **ew**. Write **long u** words to complete the sentences.

few	blue	new	true

1. A fact is _____.

2. His eyes are _____.

3. I need _____ shoes.

4. Stay a _____ minutes.

An **article** is a small word that comes before a noun. **A** and **an** are articles. Write **a** before a word that begins with a consonant letter. Write **an** before a word that begins with a vowel letter. Write **a** or **an** to complete each sentence.

1. I found _____ book.

2. It told a story about _____ ant.

3. In the story, _____ lion gave three wishes to _____ ant.

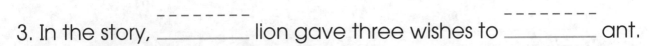

Name _____

Use the code to color the shapes.

Write the first word of each **asking sentence**. It should begin with an uppercase letter. Write a **question mark** to end each sentence.

| can | do | what |

1. _____ we feed the ducks □

2. _____ you see the monkeys □

3. _____ time will we eat lunch □

Solve the word problems.

1. At the zoo, Nina counted 6 lizards on a rock. She counted 9 lizards on a ledge. How many lizards did she count in all?   _____ lizards

2. The zoo has 17 monkeys. 5 monkeys are sleeping. How many monkeys are awake?   _____ monkeys

Say the name of each picture. Write a letter that matches its **beginning** sound, **middle** sound, and **ending** sound. Color the pictures.

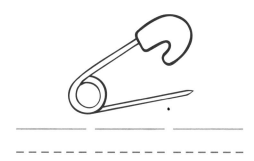

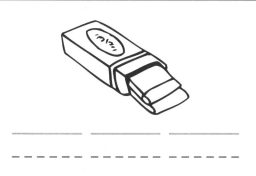

Write the missing numbers.

Write the number of **rectangles** you find in the picture. Use a different color to trace each one.

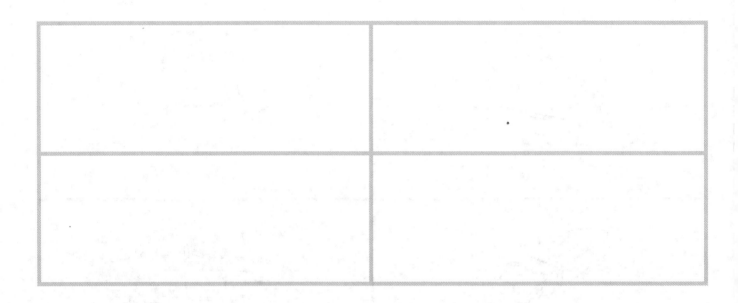

_____ rectangles

In some words, two consonant sounds blend together. This is called a **consonant blend**. Say the name of each picture. Circle its beginning consonant blend.

bl   fl   cl

cl   fl   gl

fl   bl   pl

Add. Write each sum on a spaceship.

15 + 2 =

3 + 16 =

8 + 5 =

13 + 5 =

6 + 8 =

16 + 4 =

Write the **long e** words where they belong.

| bee | wheel | keep | feel | see | cheese | deer | peek |

Nouns (Naming Words)

Verbs (Action Words)

Subtract. Write each difference on a beehive.

20 - 3 =

20 - 5 =

11 - 6 =

13 - 8 =

18 - 2 =

16 - 16 =

Say the name of each picture. Circle its beginning **consonant blend**.

fl   cl   gl

pl   gl   cl

gl   fl   sl

A **proper noun** is a name for a specific person, place, or thing. Your name is a proper noun. Proper nouns always begin with an uppercase letter. Write a proper noun to name each picture.

| Jack and Jill | Lynn Cramer | Chicago | Fluffy |

Write **>** or **<** in the circle to show which number in each pair is **greater**. Make sure the "open mouth" points to the larger number.

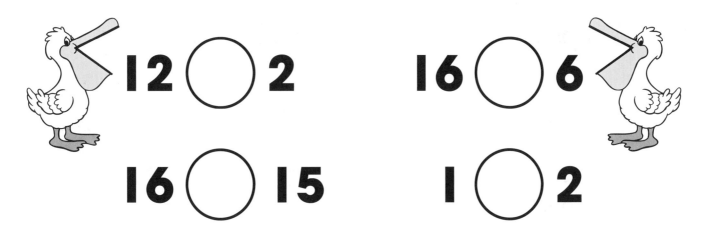

12 ◯ 2   16 ◯ 6

16 ◯ 15   1 ◯ 2

Write a **consonant blend** to begin each word.

_____ain

_____og

_____ab

Write the number that matches each group of **tens** and **ones**.

4 tens   6 ones _____   3 tens   2 ones _____

2 tens   9 ones _____   4 tens   0 ones _____

1 ten   4 ones _____   0 tens   6 ones _____

2 tens   1 one _____   4 tens   7 ones _____

3 tens   3 ones _____   1 ten   1 one _____

A **past-tense verb** tells about an action that already happened. Add **ed** to most verbs to show the past tense. Write the past tense of each verb. The first one is done for you.

1. push  pushed

2. want _____

3. help _____

4. heat _____

5. color _____

6. pull _____

Write any numbers to make the addition problems true.

_____ + _____ = 7   _____ + _____ = 9

_____ + _____ = 7   _____ + _____ = 9

_____ + _____ = 11   _____ + _____ = 12

_____ + _____ = 11   _____ + _____ = 12

Count the items in the picture. Write the numbers in the boxes. The first one is done for you.

Circle the **nouns** in each sentence. Underline the **verb** in each sentence.

1. The turtle eats leaves.

2. The fish swim in the tank.

3. The girl hits the ball.

Add and **subtract**.

15
− 1

7 + 7 = _____

18 − 4 = _____

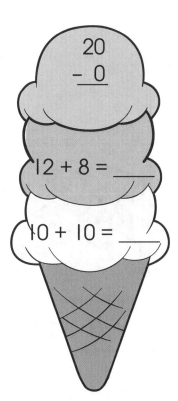

20
− 0

12 + 8 = _____

10 + 10 = _____

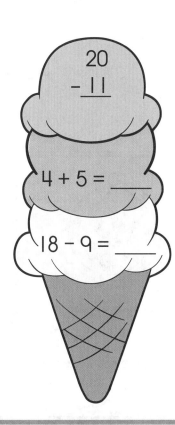

20
− 11

4 + 5 = _____

18 − 9 = _____

Use the number line to count back. Under each kangaroo, write the numbers you counted back. Then, write the difference.

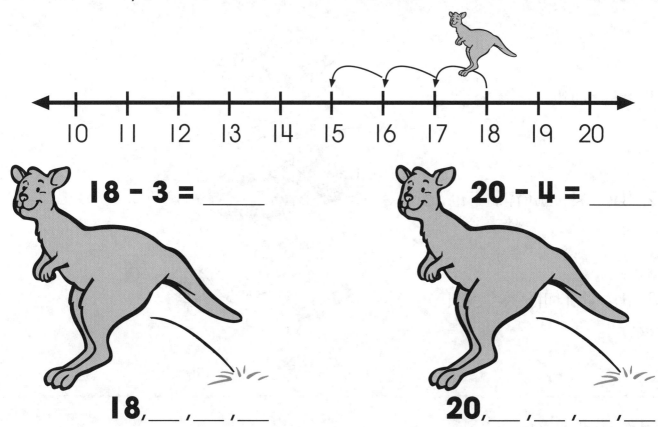

18 - 3 = _____

20 - 4 = _____

18, __ , __ , __

20, __ , __ , __ , __

Say the name of each picture. Circle its beginning **consonant blend**.

gl   fl   cl

sl   fl   cl

cl   gl   sl

Look at the foods. Color the meats **brown**. Color the fruits and vegetables **green**. Color the breads **tan**. Color the dairy foods **yellow**.

fish	bread	apple	cheese
crackers	carrot	orange	eggs
steak	pear	milk	yogurt
ice cream	chicken	potato	pretzel

A **proper noun** is a name for a specific person, place, or thing. It begins with an uppercase letter. Write a proper noun to name each picture.

Rover	Mike Smith	Utah	Sarah

_____   _____
-    -
_____   _____

_____   _____
-    -
_____   _____

Draw an X on the **first** flower. Draw a circle around the **fifth** flower. Underline the **seventh** flower. Draw a square around the **tenth** flower.

Say the name of the first picture in the row. Circle pictures whose names begin with the same sound.

chair

shell

Roll dice to find two addends. Write them on the first two lines. Then, **add** to find the sum.

1. _____ + _____ = _____

2. _____ + _____ = _____

3. _____ + _____ = _____

4. _____ + _____ = _____

Most **past-tense verbs** end with **ed**. Write the past tense of the verb in each sentence.

1. I _____ Mom a gift.
(hand)

2. She _____ it quickly.
(open)

3. Mom _____ surprised.
(look)

Write **>** or **<** in the circle to show which number in each pair is **greater**. Make sure the "open mouth" points to the larger number.

7 ◯ 1

9 ◯ 6

19 ◯ 5

11 ◯ 13

Subtract.

11 − 9	12 − 6	13 − 9	9 − 4	15 − 7

14 − 9	14 − 7	8 − 5	11 − 2	14 − 8

Write a **consonant blend** to begin each word.

_____um

_____ush

_____esent

Say the name of each picture. Draw a line to its beginning **consonant blend**.

sk

sm

sw

Add.

2 +9	6 +6	4 +9	5 +4	8 +7

5 +9	7 +7	3 +5	9 +9	7 +9

Write an **adjective** to describe each animal.

green	bushy	six

1. A  has a _____ tail.

2. A  has _____ legs.

3. The  will become a _____ frog.

Write the number of **triangles** you find in the picture. Use a different color to trace each one.

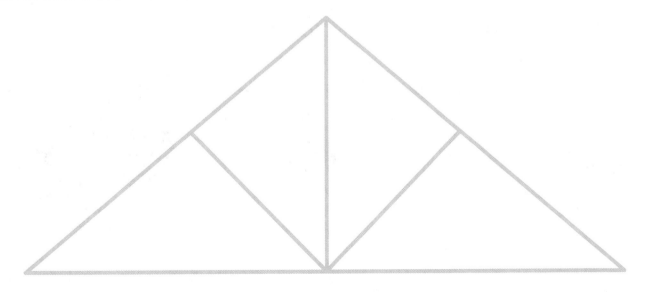

_____ triangles

Write how many **tens** and **ones** are in each number.

                tens   **ones**

28 = _____ tens, _____ ones

64 = _____ tens, _____ ones

56 = _____ tens, _____ ones

72 = _____ tens, _____ ones

38 = _____ tens, _____ ones

17 = _____ ten, _____ ones

63 = _____ tens, _____ ones

Write **lt** or **ft** to complete each word.

ra_____

sa_____

le_____

An **article** is a small word that comes before a noun. **A** and **an** are articles. Write **a** before a word that begins with a consonant sound. Write **an** before a word that begins with a vowel sound. Write **a** or **an** to complete each sentence.

1. The ant's first wish was to ride _____ elephant.

2. The second wish was to ride _____ alligator.

3. The last wish was _____ wish for three more wishes.

Solve the word problems.

1. Jace walked 9 steps to the swings. He walked 8 steps to the slide. How many steps did he walk in all?

_____ steps

2. Lizzie's book has 18 pages. She read 3 pages. How many pages does she have left to read?

_____ pages

Say the name of the first picture in the row. Circle pictures whose names begin with the same sound.

thumb

wheel

When the long hand is on 6, the clock shows a **half-hour**. The hour is the number that the short hand just passed. The minutes are **:30**. Write the time shown on each clock. The first one is done for you.

4:00   4:30   _____   _____

Read the clues. Write the words.

rake	way	mail	save

If you can spell **take**, then you can spell

_____

- -

_____ .

If you can spell **gave**, then you can spell

_____

- -

_____ .

If you can spell **may**, then you can spell

_____

- -

_____ .

If you can spell **nail**, then you can spell

_____

- -

_____ .

Write the missing numbers to make the subtraction problems true.

$$15 - \square = 2$$

$$18 - \square = 4$$

$$19 - \square = 6$$

$$\square - 13 = 6$$

$$\square - 18 = 1$$

$$\square - 14 = 5$$

$$16 - \square = 3$$

$$\square - 13 = 5$$

The sentences tell about yesterday. Choose the **past-tense verb** to write in each blank.

1. We _____ water to the paint.
   (add, added)

2. I _____ yellow and blue.
   (mixed, mix)

3. I _____ a bird.
   (painted, paint)

4. I _____ my brush.
   (clean, cleaned)

Number the boxes **1**, **2**, **3** to put the story in order.

_____   _____   _____

Say the name of each picture. Draw a line to its ending **consonant blend**.

sk

lk

st

Solve the word problems.

1. On a plate, Mom put 8 apple slices and 5 orange slices. How many fruit slices were on the plate?

   _____ slices

2. **Butterfly** has 9 letters. **Ladybug** has 7 letters. How many more letters does **butterfly** have?

   _____ letters

Write an **adjective** to describe each animal.

| round | big | three |

1. A 🦫 has _____ teeth.

2. _____ 🦇 hang by their tails.

3. An 🦉 has _____ eyes.

Circle the equations that are true. Draw an X through equations that are not true.

$$\begin{array}{r} 8 \\ +\ 8 \\ \hline 16 \end{array} \qquad \begin{array}{r} 20 \\ -\ 4 \\ \hline 15 \end{array} \qquad \begin{array}{r} 17 \\ +\ 2 \\ \hline 19 \end{array} \qquad \begin{array}{r} 18 \\ -\ 7 \\ \hline 9 \end{array}$$

$$\begin{array}{r} 6 \\ +\ 6 \\ \hline 14 \end{array} \qquad \begin{array}{r} 13 \\ -\ 5 \\ \hline 8 \end{array} \qquad \begin{array}{r} 10 \\ +\ 6 \\ \hline 16 \end{array} \qquad \begin{array}{r} 11 \\ -\ 3 \\ \hline 8 \end{array}$$

Say the name of each picture. Draw a line to its beginning
consonant blend.

sn

sp

sl

Each clock shows a time half past the hour. Write the time.

___ : ___   ___ : ___   ___ : ___   ___ : ___

Add.

9	6	8	9	9
+8	+5	+5	+6	+4

4	8	9	4	4
+4	+6	+7	+8	+7

Write **It** or **If** to complete each word.

qui_____

be_____

she_____

Look at the graph. Answer the questions.

Favorite Foods

10				
9				
8				
7				
6				
5				
4				
3				
2				
1				

 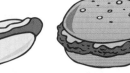 

hot dog   **hamburger**   **pizza**   **chicken**

1. How many people like pizza best? _____

2. How many people like chicken best? _____

3. Which food do most people like best? _____

4. Which food do the fewest number of people like best? _____

Circle the correct **verb** to complete each sentence.

1. The bear (climb, climbs) a ladder.

2. Two tiny dogs (dance, dances).

3. A boy (eat, eats) popcorn.

4. A woman (swing, swings) on a trapeze.

Trace three paths from **A** to **B**. Trace each path with a different color.

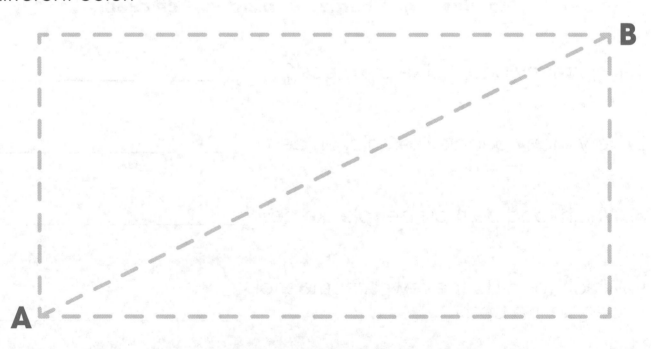

Add each beginning letter to the word ending to write new words.

___ and

b _____

h _____

l _____

s _____

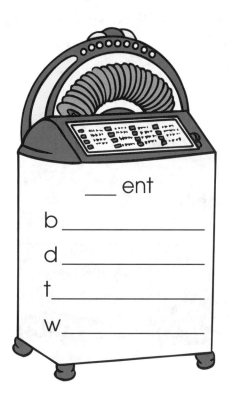

___ ent

b _____

d _____

t _____

w _____

Subtract.

17	11	13	15	13
− 1	− 5	− 5	− 6	− 4

8	14	16	12	11
− 4	− 6	− 7	− 8	− 7

In some words, two or three consonant letters make one sound. This is called a **consonant digraph**. Say the name of the picture at the beginning of the row. Circle pictures whose names have the same sound.

whistle

shoe

Write a **period** at the end of each **telling sentence**. Write a **question mark** at the end of each **asking sentence**.

1. What would you like to do first

2. Do you want to see the ducks

3. There are four of them on the pond

4. We will see the baby chicks next

Rewrite the number of **tens** and **ones**. Then, write the number. The first one is done for you.

	tens	ones		
3 tens, 2 ones	3	2	=	32
3 tens, 7 ones	____	____	=	____
9 tens, 1 one	____	____	=	____
5 tens, 6 ones	____	____	=	____
6 tens, 5 ones	____	____	=	____

Solve the word problems.

1. 6 first-grade girls were absent on Monday. 7 first-grade boys were absent on Monday. How many first graders were absent on Monday?

   _____ first graders

2. Ms. Willey's paper was 18 inches long. She cut off 3 inches. How long is the paper now?

   _____ inches

Circle the correct **verb** to complete each sentence.

1. Children (swim, swims) in the pool.

2. The car (race, races) around the track.

3. Mike (throw, throws) the ball to his friend.

4. Monkeys (swing, swings) in the trees.

Circle the equations that are true. Draw an X through equations that are not true.

$$\begin{array}{r} 13 \\ -\ 4 \\ \hline 9 \end{array} \qquad \begin{array}{r} 10 \\ -10 \\ \hline 20 \end{array} \qquad \begin{array}{r} 10 \\ -\ 2 \\ \hline 8 \end{array} \qquad \begin{array}{r} 16 \\ +\ 2 \\ \hline 19 \end{array}$$

$$\begin{array}{r} 10 \\ -\ 7 \\ \hline 3 \end{array} \qquad \begin{array}{r} 20 \\ -\ 5 \\ \hline 15 \end{array} \qquad \begin{array}{r} 11 \\ -\ 1 \\ \hline 10 \end{array} \qquad \begin{array}{r} 20 \\ +\ 0 \\ \hline 19 \end{array}$$

Write the name of each picture. Underline the **consonant digraph** (two consonant letters that make a single sound) in each word.

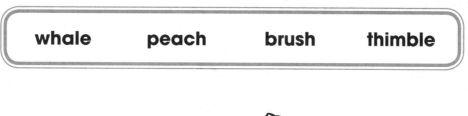

| whale | peach | brush | thimble |

 _____

 _____

 _____

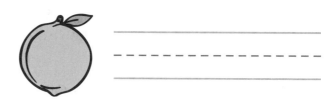 _____

Each clock shows a time half past the hour. Write the time.

___:___   ___:___   ___:___   ___:___

Rewrite the dates. Begin the name of each month with an uppercase letter. Use a **comma** to separate the day and the year. The first one is done for you.

1. On april 17 2005, we saw the Grand Canyon.

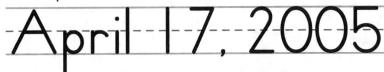
April 17, 2005

2. Our vacation started on april 2 2002.

3. Molly's sister was born on august 14 2011.

Add.

$$\begin{array}{r} 4 \\ +6 \\ \hline \end{array} \qquad \begin{array}{r} 5 \\ +3 \\ \hline \end{array} \qquad \begin{array}{r} 4 \\ +5 \\ \hline \end{array} \qquad \begin{array}{r} 9 \\ +9 \\ \hline \end{array} \qquad \begin{array}{r} 7 \\ +3 \\ \hline \end{array}$$

$$\begin{array}{r} 6 \\ +6 \\ \hline \end{array} \qquad \begin{array}{r} 7 \\ +8 \\ \hline \end{array} \qquad \begin{array}{r} 3 \\ +8 \\ \hline \end{array} \qquad \begin{array}{r} 6 \\ +3 \\ \hline \end{array} \qquad \begin{array}{r} 2 \\ +6 \\ \hline \end{array}$$

Say the name of the picture at the beginning of the row. Circle pictures whose names begin with the same sound.

chin

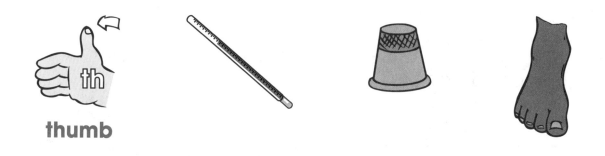

thumb

Cut a piece of string as long as your pencil. Use the string to measure things. In the chart, list the things you measured.

Shorter	Same	Longer

The sentences tell about yesterday. Choose the **past-tense verb** to write in each blank.

1. Jill _____ an egg into the bowl.
   (cracked, cracks)

2. She _____ in a little milk and vanilla.
   (pours, poured)

3. Jill _____ the batter into a cake pan.
   (spooned, spoons)

4. She _____ it for 35 minutes.
   (bakes, baked)

Subtract.

$$\begin{array}{r} 10 \\ -\ 6 \\ \hline \end{array} \qquad \begin{array}{r} 8 \\ -3 \\ \hline \end{array} \qquad \begin{array}{r} 9 \\ -5 \\ \hline \end{array} \qquad \begin{array}{r} 18 \\ -9 \\ \hline \end{array} \qquad \begin{array}{r} 10 \\ -\ 3 \\ \hline \end{array}$$

$$\begin{array}{r} 14 \\ -\ 8 \\ \hline \end{array} \qquad \begin{array}{r} 15 \\ -\ 8 \\ \hline \end{array} \qquad \begin{array}{r} 11 \\ -\ 8 \\ \hline \end{array} \qquad \begin{array}{r} 9 \\ -3 \\ \hline \end{array} \qquad \begin{array}{r} 8 \\ -6 \\ \hline \end{array}$$

Rewrite the number of **tens** and **ones**. Then, write the number.
The first one is done for you.

	tens	ones		
6 tens, 8 ones	6	8	=	68
2 tens, 8 ones	___	___	=	___
4 tens, 9 ones	___	___	=	___
1 ten, 4 ones	___	___	=	___
8 tens, 2 ones	___	___	=	___

Write the name of each picture. Underline the **consonant digraph**
(two or three consonant letters that make a single sound).

watch	shoe	bench	teeth

 - - - - - - - - - - - -

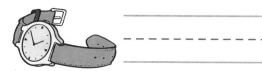 - - - - - - - - - - - -

 - - - - - - - - - - - -

 - - - - - - - - - - - -

Use a penny to measure each object.

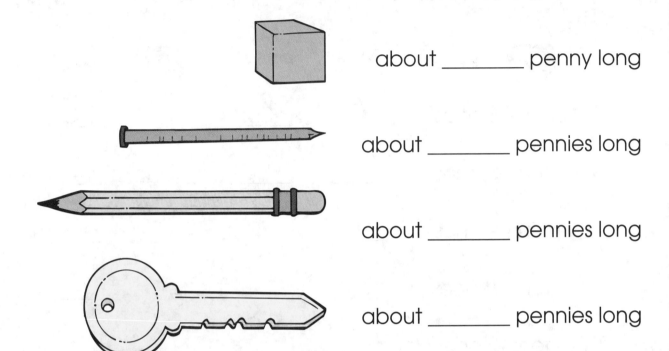

about _____ penny long

about _____ pennies long

about _____ pennies long

about _____ pennies long

Solve the word problems.

1. 15 birds were at the feeder today. 8 birds were at the feeder yesterday. How many more birds were at the feeder today?

_____ birds

2. The Wildcats scored 12 points in the first half. They scored 4 points in the second half. How many points did they score in all?

_____ points

Circle the word that is spelled correctly. Write it on the line.

rum
run
runn
_____

jump
jumb
junp
_____

mack
maek
make
_____

Say the name of each picture. Circle the **consonant digraph** you hear. Color the pictures.

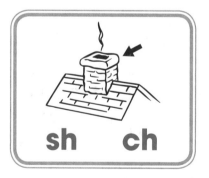
sh   ch

wh   th

ch   sh

wh   th

sh   ch

tch   sh

Add each beginning letter to the word ending to write new words.

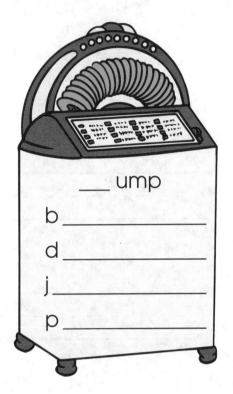

___ ump

b _____

d _____

j _____

p _____

___ ink

p _____

s _____

l _____

th _____

Draw hands on each clock to show a **half-hour**.

2:30

4:30

1:30

A **preposition** is a word that can tell **where** something is. In a sentence, it shows the relationship between two nouns or pronouns. Some prepositions that tell where are **in**, **inside**, **on**, **near**, and **around**. In each sentence, look at the underlined nouns. Circle a preposition that tells where.

1. The <u>plates</u> in the <u>cupboard</u> were clean.

2. Put the <u>card</u> inside the <u>envelope</u>.

3. The <u>towel</u> on the <u>sink</u> was wet.

4. The <u>chair</u> near the <u>counter</u> was sticky.

5. I put the <u>bow</u> around the <u>box</u>.

Trace the path from **A** to **B**.

How many corners did you turn? _____

Color words and number words are **adjectives**. Underline the describing word in each sentence. Draw a picture for each sentence.

Three apples grew on the tree.

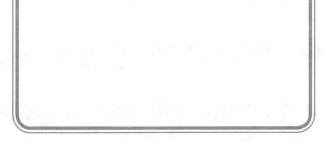

The girl wore a blue dress.

Circle the equations that are true. Draw an X through equations that are not true.

$$\begin{array}{r} 20 \\ -0 \\ \hline 18 \end{array} \qquad \begin{array}{r} 5 \\ +4 \\ \hline 9 \end{array} \qquad \begin{array}{r} 17 \\ +3 \\ \hline 20 \end{array} \qquad \begin{array}{r} 18 \\ -11 \\ \hline 7 \end{array}$$

$$\begin{array}{r} 12 \\ -8 \\ \hline 4 \end{array} \qquad \begin{array}{r} 11 \\ +7 \\ \hline 17 \end{array} \qquad \begin{array}{r} 10 \\ -4 \\ \hline 6 \end{array} \qquad \begin{array}{r} 14 \\ +3 \\ \hline 17 \end{array}$$

Trace each shape. Draw another example of each shape.

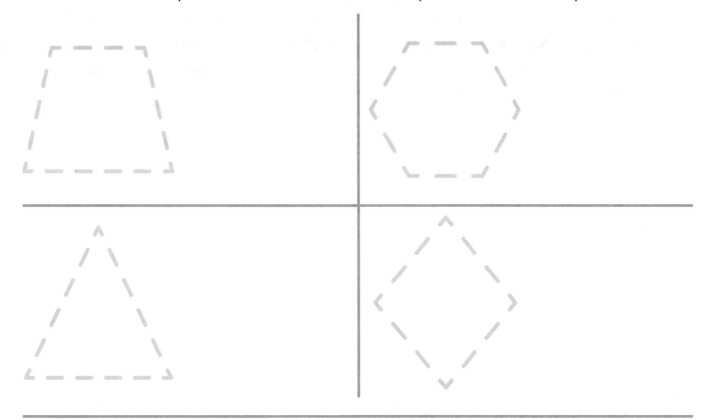

Say the name of each picture. Circle the **consonant digraph** you hear. Color the pictures.

sh   ch

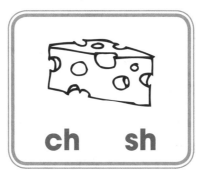

ch   sh

wh   th

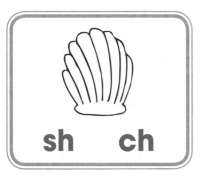

sh   ch

ch   sh

wh   th

Write the words in the correct columns.

| car | house | boat | plane | cow | window |
| girl | hen | bird | dog | tree | rocks |

Living

1. _____
2. _____
3. _____
4. _____
5. _____
6. _____

Non-Living

1. _____
2. _____
3. _____
4. _____
5. _____
6. _____

Use a penny to measure each object.

about _____ pennies long

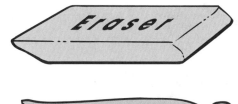

about _____ pennies long

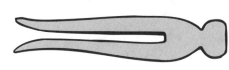

about _____ pennies long

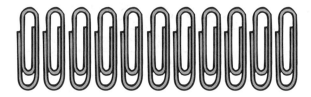

about _____ pennies long

Add. Draw pictures to help. The first one is done for you.

```
  1 ○
  2 ○ ○
+ 3 ○ ○ ○
─────
  6
```

```
  3
  6
+ 2
───
```

```
  8
  5
+ 4
───
```

```
  3
  1
+ 5
───
```

Rewrite the dates. Begin the name of each month with an uppercase letter. Use a **comma** to separate the day and the year. The first one is done for you.

1. My father's birthday is may 19 1978.

May 19, 1978

2. My sister was fourteen on december 13 2012.

_____

_____

3. Lauren's seventh birthday was on november 30 2010.

_____

_____

4. october 13 2013 was the last day I saw my lost cat.

_____

_____

Each clock shows a **half-hour**. Write the time.

_____   _____   _____

Say the name of each picture. Write the first two letters on the line.

Add three numbers to solve the word problems.

1. Marty had 3 marbles. Jake had 7 marbles.
   John had 4 marbles. How many marbles
   did the boys have altogether?

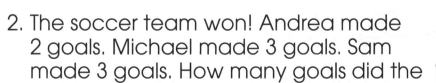

   _____ marbles

2. The soccer team won! Andrea made
   2 goals. Michael made 3 goals. Sam
   made 3 goals. How many goals did the
   soccer team make?

   _____ goals

To add three numbers, first look for two numbers with a sum of 10. Then, add the third number. **Add**. The first one is done for you.

$$\begin{array}{r} 7 \\ 3 \\ + 4 \\ \hline 14 \end{array} \Big\} 10$$

$$\begin{array}{r} 2 \\ 6 \\ + 8 \\ \hline \end{array}$$

$$\begin{array}{r} 6 \\ 8 \\ + 4 \\ \hline \end{array}$$

$$\begin{array}{r} 9 \\ 7 \\ + 1 \\ \hline \end{array}$$

Look at the objects. For each sentence, circle **True** or **False**.

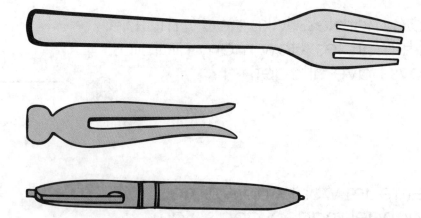

1. The clothespin is longer than the pen.   **True**   **False**

2. The pen is shorter than the fork.   **True**   **False**

3. The fork is longer than the clothespin.   **True**   **False**

Name _____

On each line, write a **proper noun** that names something about you. Begin each one with an uppercase letter.

1. Your first name: _____

2. Your last name: _____

3. Your street: _____

4. Your city: _____

5. Your state: _____

Say each word. Write it under the letters you hear at the end.

| long | bank | stung | honk | bunk | sang |

ŏng

nk

_____

_____

Color the ☆s yellow. Color the ○s **red**. Color the ☾s **blue**. Color the ◇s **purple**. Write the number you count for each shape.

How many stars? _____   How many moons? _____

How many circles? _____   How many rhombuses? _____

A **possessive pronoun** shows ownership. Rewrite the sentences with the possessive pronoun in place of the **bold** words.

1. That is **Lisa's** book. (her)

_____

- -

_____

2. This is **my pencil**. (mine)

_____

- -

_____

Say the name of each picture. Then, write a **rhyming** word.

| chop | chain | chin | chase |

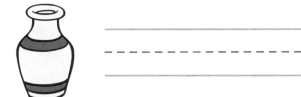

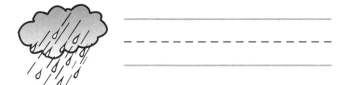

How many different shapes can you find in the picture? Trace each shape with a different color.

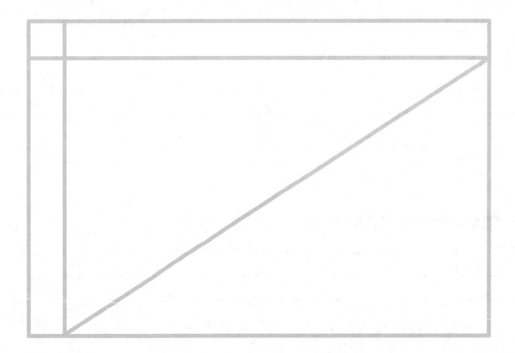

Add. Draw pictures to help. The first one is done for you.

$$1 \; \bigcirc$$
$$2 \; \bigcirc \; \bigcirc$$
$$+3 \; \bigcirc \; \bigcirc \; \bigcirc$$
$$\overline{6}$$

$$8$$
$$2$$
$$+9$$
$$\overline{}$$

$$9$$
$$4$$
$$+2$$
$$\overline{}$$

$$3$$
$$7$$
$$+6$$
$$\overline{}$$

Write the category that describes each group of words.

clothes	flowers	colors

rose
buttercup
tulip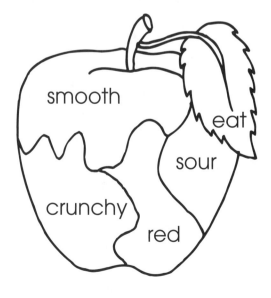
daisy

_____

green
purple
blue
red

_____

shirt
socks
dress
coat

_____

Color each space that has an **adjective**, or describing word.

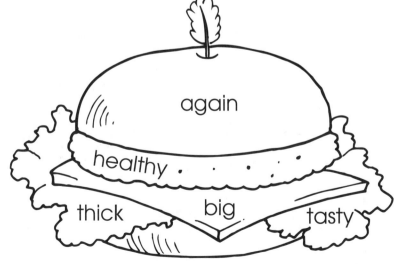

smooth
eat
sour
crunchy
red

again
healthy
thick
big
tasty

Add three numbers to solve the word problems.

1. The first grade ran in three races. Team A scored 5 points. Team B scored 6 points. Team C scored 8 points. How many points did the first grade score?

_____ points

2. We went to the farm. We saw 6 black pigs. We saw 4 black and white cows. We saw 6 brown hens. How many animals did we see at the farm?

_____ animals

Say the name of each picture. Write the first two letters on the line.

_ _ _ _ _ _ _ _

_ _ _ _ _ _ _ _

_ _ _ _ _ _ _ _

Draw lines to match clocks that show the same time.

1:30

3:30

10:30

Write a word to complete each sentence.

| whale | which | where |

1. _____ are we going this afternoon?

2. _____ red dress will Wendy buy?

3. A huge _____ swam near the shore.

Add each beginning letter to the word ending to write new words.

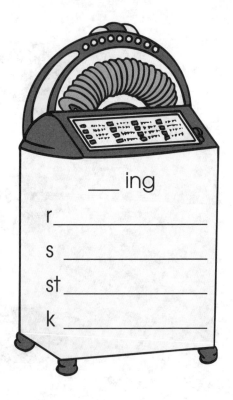

___ing

r_____

s _____

st_____

k _____

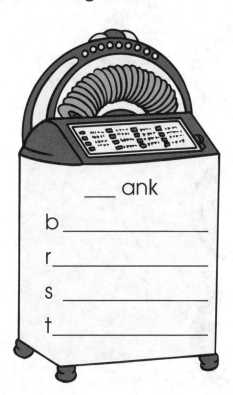

___ank

b_____

r_____

s _____

t_____

Color to complete the patterns.

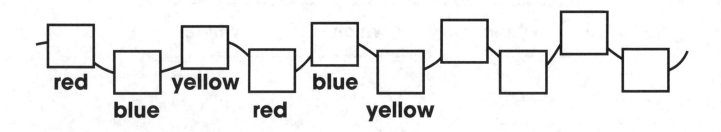

red   blue   yellow   red   blue   yellow

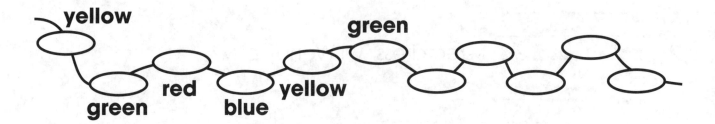

yellow   green   red   blue   yellow   green

Look for two numbers with a sum of 10. Then, add the third number.
Add. The first one is done for you.

$$\begin{array}{r} 8 \\ 4 \\ + 6 \\ \hline 18 \end{array} \Big\} 10$$

$$\begin{array}{r} 1 \\ 5 \\ + 9 \\ \hline \end{array}$$

$$\begin{array}{r} 7 \\ 4 \\ + 3 \\ \hline \end{array}$$

$$\begin{array}{r} 2 \\ 9 \\ + 8 \\ \hline \end{array}$$

An **exclamation** is a sentence that shows excitement. It ends with an **exclamation mark** (**!**). Write **.**, **?**, or **!** to end each sentence.

1. Where is the bottom of the hill ☐

2. It is fun to zoom down ☐

3. The penguin's skis are red ☐

4. Skiing is so much fun ☐

To add three numbers, first add any doubles. Then, add the third number. **Add**. The first one is done for you.

```
  8
  3
+ 3  ⟩6
  14
```

```
  5
  5
+ 4
```

```
  7
  1
+ 7
```

```
  6
  2
+ 6
```

Draw an X on the picture that does not belong in each group.

fruit

apple　　　peach　　　corn　　　watermelon

wild animals

bear　　　kitten　　　gorilla　　　lion

Choose a **verb** to complete each sentence.

draw	write	helps	delivers
help	deliver	draws	writes

1. I _____ a newspaper about our street.

2. My sister _____ me sometimes.

3. She _____ the pictures.

4. We _____ them together.

Draw a line to the correct number.

4 tens + 7 ones   20

2 tens + 0 ones   51

7 tens + 3 ones   47

5 tens + 1 one   73

Add three numbers to solve the word problems.

1. Mother picked flowers from the garden. She picked 7 pansies, 4 irises, and 3 daffodils. How many flowers did Mother pick?

_____ flowers

2. Spot ate 6 dog treats. Rover ate 4 dog treats. Wags ate 5 dog treats. How many treats did the dogs eat altogether?

_____ treats

Look at the objects. For each sentence, circle **True** or **False**.

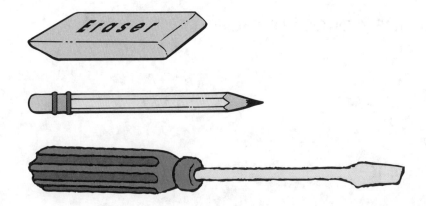

1. The pencil is longer than the screwdriver.   **True**   **False**

2. The eraser is shorter than the pencil.   **True**   **False**

3. The screwdriver is the longest object.   **True**   **False**

Write each word under a category.

carrots	cherries	chicken	cheese	fish	ham
cake	lettuce	bagel	oranges	pears	rolls
beans	milk	toast	pie	candy bar	yogurt

GRAINS

VEGETABLES

FRUITS

DAIRY

SWEETS

MEATS

Say each **long vowel** word. Write a vowel letter to complete it.

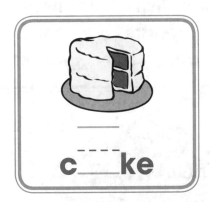
c__ke

h__ke

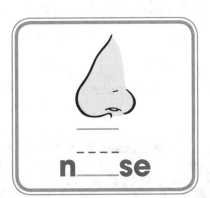
n__se

c__be

gr__pes

k__te

Write the number that is:

next   **one less**   **one greater**

68, 69, _____   _____, 57   12, _____

86, 87, _____   _____, 50   43, _____

First, add any doubles. Then, add the third number. **Add**. The first one is done for you.

$$\begin{array}{r} 4 \\ 4 \end{array}\!\!\Big\rangle 8$$
$$\underline{+\ 5}$$
$$13$$

$$\begin{array}{r} 2 \\ 9 \\ \underline{+\ 2} \end{array}$$

$$\begin{array}{r} 8 \\ 3 \\ \underline{+\ 8} \end{array}$$

$$\begin{array}{r} 9 \\ 2 \\ \underline{+\ 9} \end{array}$$

Make a check mark beside each **proper noun**.

_____ uncle

_____ school

_____ Aunt Retta

_____ Miss Hunter

_____ Forest Park

_____ Union Station

_____ Missouri

_____ shopping mall

Unscramble the words. In each word, the **long vowel sound** is spelled with two vowel letters together.

 ocat _____

 eetf _____

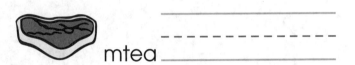 mtea _____

 apil _____

Complete the number patterns.

1. 5, _____ , _____ , 20, _____ , _____ , 35, _____ , _____ , 50

2. _____ , 4, 6, _____ , _____ , 12, _____ , 16, _____ , _____

3. 10, _____ , _____ , 40, _____ , _____ , 70, _____ , 90

4. 4, _____ , 12, _____ , _____ , 24, _____ , 32, _____ , 40

Add. Break up each problem into two smaller problems. The first one is done for you.

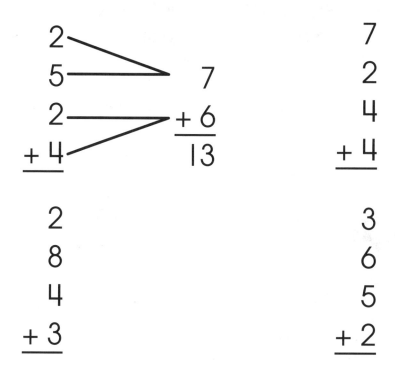

```
  2                    7
  5      7            2
  2    + 6           4
+ 4     13          + 4


  2                   3
  8                   6
  4                   5
+ 3                 + 2
```

A **possessive pronoun** shows ownership. Rewrite the sentences with the possessive pronoun in place of the **bold** words.

1. This hat is **your hat**. (yours)

_____

- -

_____

2. Fifi is **Kevin's** cat. (his)

_____

- -

_____

Write the category that describes each group of words.

| animals | toys | fruits |

puzzle
wagon
blocks
doll
_____
- - - - - - - - - - -
_____

grapes
orange
apple
plum
_____
- - - - - - - - - - -
_____

dog
horse
elephant
moose
_____
- - - - - - - - - - -
_____

Write a number to show how many dots in all.

_____ dots

Count the tally marks. Write the number.

(卌 卌) III   _____   (卌 卌)(卌 卌)   _____

(卌 卌) 卌 II   _____   卌 III   _____

Use tally marks to represent the numbers.

15 [ ]   **22** [ ]

A **command** is a sentence that tells what to do. It begins with a **verb**. A command can end with a period (**.**) or an exclamation mark (**!**). Underline each sentence that gives a command.

Look over there. Mari is running fast. She has the ball. Shoot the ball, Mari!

Add. Break up each problem into two smaller problems. The first one is done for you.

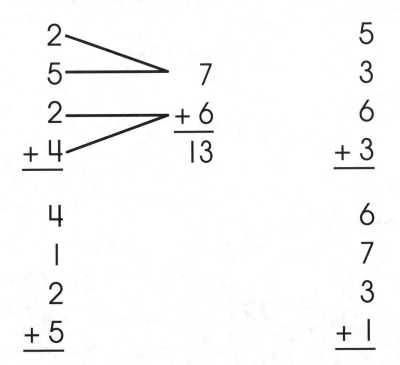

```
2           5
5    7      3
2  + 6      6
+4   13    +3


4           6
1           7
2           3
+5         +1
```

Choose a **preposition** to complete each sentence. Write it in the boxes.

| before | after | next |

1. I went home _____ my soccer game.

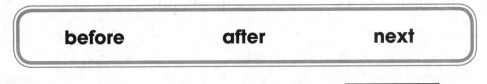

2. Can I sit _____ to you?

3. We got a treat _____ the show.

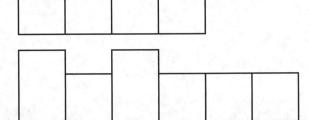

Write a word to answer each riddle.

| blow | slipper | clock |

1. People use me to tell the time. **What am I?**

_____

2. Cinderella lost one like me at midnight. **What am I?**

_____

3. You can do this with a whistle or with bubblegum. **What am I?**

_____

Write or draw what comes next in each pattern.

1.

2. A, 1, B, 2, C, _____

3. 2, 4, 6, 8, _____

Subtract.

$$\begin{array}{r} 11 \\ -\ 3 \\ \hline \end{array} \qquad \begin{array}{r} 14 \\ -\ 4 \\ \hline \end{array} \qquad \begin{array}{r} 13 \\ -\ 7 \\ \hline \end{array} \qquad \begin{array}{r} 5 \\ -\ 2 \\ \hline \end{array} \qquad \begin{array}{r} 12 \\ -\ 5 \\ \hline \end{array}$$

$$\begin{array}{r} 7 \\ -\ 4 \\ \hline \end{array} \qquad \begin{array}{r} 16 \\ -\ 8 \\ \hline \end{array} \qquad \begin{array}{r} 7 \\ -\ 2 \\ \hline \end{array} \qquad \begin{array}{r} 12 \\ -\ 9 \\ \hline \end{array} \qquad \begin{array}{r} 11 \\ -\ 6 \\ \hline \end{array}$$

Write **>** or **<** in the circle to show which number in each pair is **greater**. Make sure the "open mouth" points to the larger number.

36 ◯ 49   35 ◯ 53

20 ◯ 18   74 ◯ 21

Write each word in the correct row.

airplane   drum   radio   plate   car   pencil

spoon   crayon   chalk   fork   television   boat

Things we ride in:

_____

Things we eat with:

_____

Things we draw with:

_____

Things we listen to:

_____

Fill in the missing letters to spell each word twice.

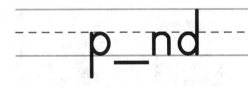  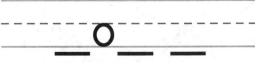

Add.

8	4	6	3	7
+3	+4	+7	+2	+5

3	8	5	3	6
+4	+8	+2	+9	+8

Say each word and decide if it has a **short vowel sound** or a **long vowel sound**. Write it under the correct category.

| bone | blink | toast | doll | wild | soft |

Short Vowel Sound

- - - - - - - - - - - - - - - - -

- - - - - - - - - - - - - - - - -

- - - - - - - - - - - - - - - - -

Long Vowel Sound

- - - - - - - - - - - - - - - - -

- - - - - - - - - - - - - - - - -

- - - - - - - - - - - - - - - - -

Circle the longest object. Draw an X on the shortest object.

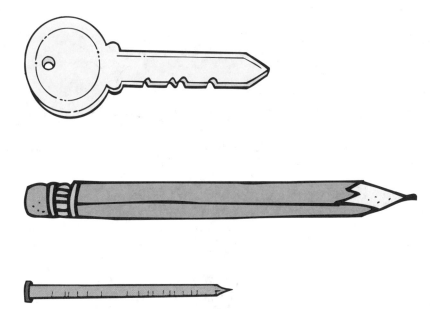

A **possessive pronoun** shows ownership. Rewrite each sentence with the possessive pronoun in place of the **bold** words.

1. That yellow house is **our home**. (ours)

   _____

   -

   _____

2. **The gerbil's** cage is too small. (Its)

   _____

   -

   _____

Write how many **tens** and **ones**. Then, write the sum. The first one is done for you.

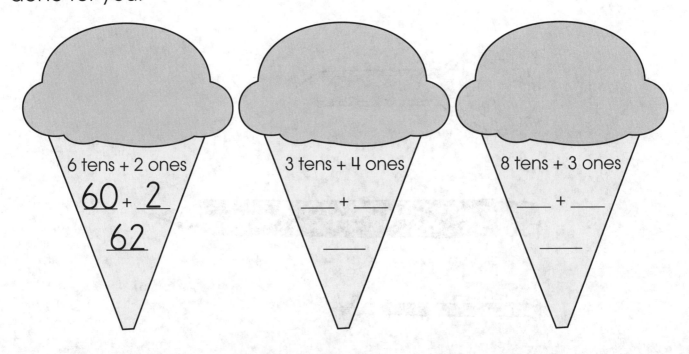

6 tens + 2 ones
60 + 2
62

3 tens + 4 ones
___ + ___
___

8 tens + 3 ones
___ + ___
___

Use a penny to measure things. What is about three pennies long? Four pennies long? Five pennies long? Fill in the chart with the names of things you measured.

Draw an X on the picture that does not belong in each group.

pets

cat   fish   elephant   dog

flowers

grass   rose   daisy   tulip

Color the boxes to show how many apples were eaten.

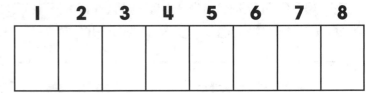

1	2	3	4	5	6	7	8

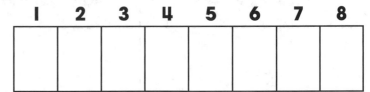

1	2	3	4	5	6	7	8

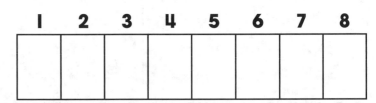

1	2	3	4	5	6	7	8

what	rush	when	shoe
ship	cash	sheep	while

1. Write the words that begin like **shark**.

2. Write the words that begin like **whistle**.

3. Write the words that end like **brush**.

Write a number for each group of **tens**. The first one is done for you.

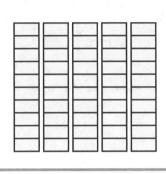 <u>50</u> 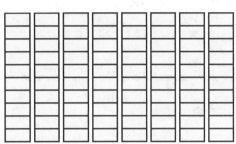 ____

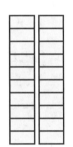 ____ 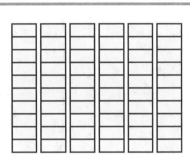 ____

Finish writing the name of each animal. Draw a line from the first part of each sentence to the part that completes it. Write a period (**.**) at the end of each sentence.

1. My friend's _c_____

                      climbs trees ☐

2. Pat's _f_____

                      sits on his finger ☐

3. The little _b_____

                      swims in the water ☐

Write the category that describes each group of words.

family	noises	coins

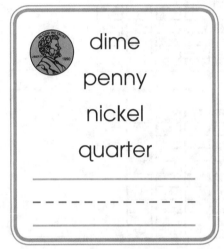
dime
penny
nickel
quarter
_____
- - - - - - - - - - -
_____

mother
father
sister
brother
_____
- - - - - - - - - - -
_____

crash
bang
ring
pop
_____
- - - - - - - - - - -
_____

Number the trees in order from **1** to **5**. Write **1** under the tallest tree.
Write **5** under the shortest tree.

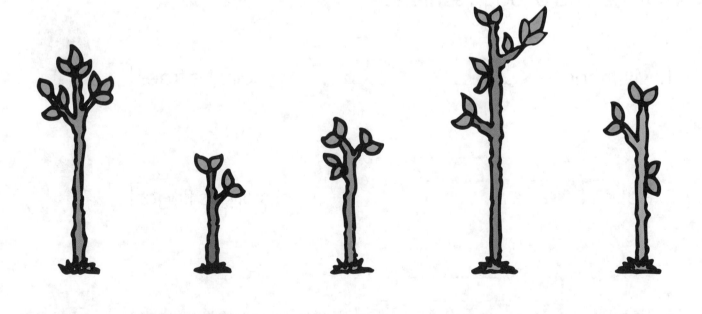

_____   _____   _____   _____   _____

Color the spaces with **telling sentences black**. Color the spaces with **asking sentences** yellow.

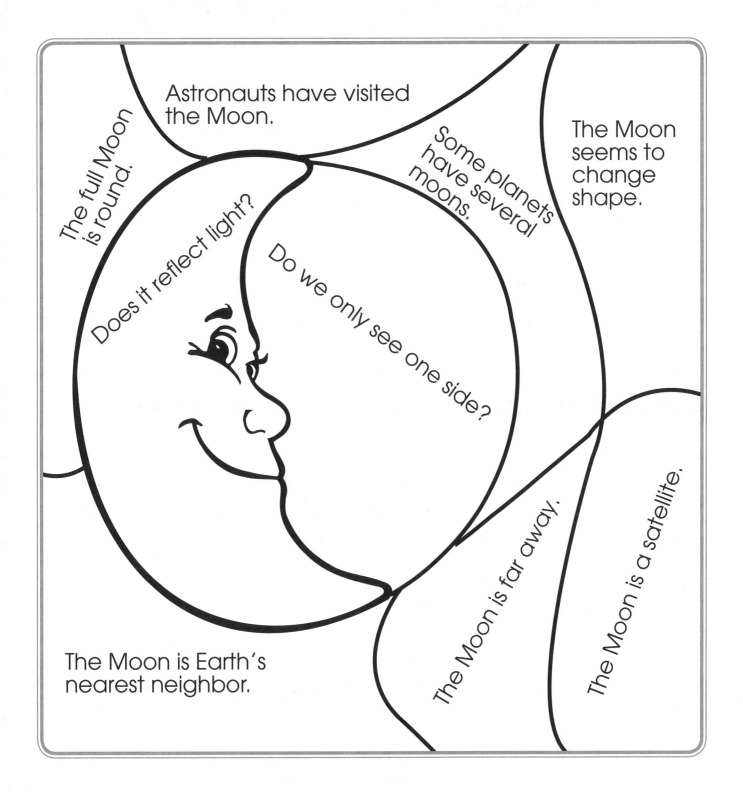

Astronauts have visited the Moon.

The full Moon is round.

Does it reflect light?

Some planets have several moons.

The Moon seems to change shape.

Do we only see one side?

The Moon is far away.

The Moon is a satellite.

The Moon is Earth's nearest neighbor.

Write a word to complete each sentence.

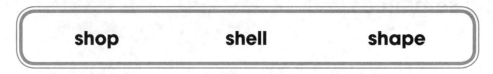

| shop | shell | shape |

1. A square is a _____ that has four equal sides.

2. Does she like to _____ at the mall?

3. The clam always stays inside its _____.

Write the circled numbers in the correct order on the lines.

0 1 2 3 4 ⑤ 6 7 8 9 10 11 ⑫ 13 14 15 16 17 18 19 20

_____ > _____

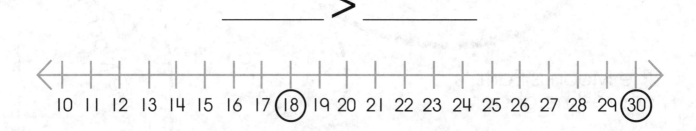

10 11 12 13 14 15 16 17 ⑱ 19 20 21 22 23 24 25 26 27 28 29 ㉚

_____ > _____

Draw glasses on the **second** child. Draw a hat on the **fourth** child. Color red hair on the **third** child. Color black hair on the **seventh** child. Draw a necktie on the **first** child. Draw a hair bow on the **sixth** child.

Write **1** on the longest fish. Write **2** on the next-longest fish. Write **3** on the shortest fish.

Circle the longest object. Draw an X on the shortest object.

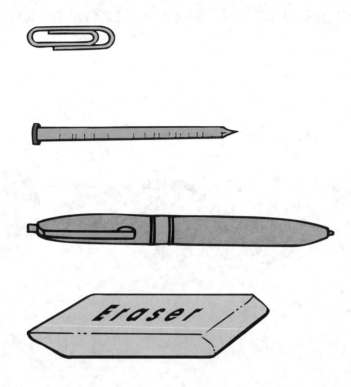

Solve the word problems.

1. The children in the Washington family are 12 years old, 8 years old, and 3 years old. What is the total of their ages?

_____ years

2. Dad made 18 muffins. 12 muffins were eaten. How many muffins were left?

_____ muffins

Use the words to complete the crossword puzzle.

chop   chin   cheek   check   chain   children   child   chase

Across

3. They will use a ___ to pull the car.

5. Many ___ like to go to the circus.

6. Write a ___ mark in the correct box.

Down

1. The baby spilled food on his ___.

2. Only one ___ is on the slide.

4. They like to run and ___ each other.

6. Dad will ___ the stump into logs.

7. The kitten licked the girl's ___.

Find the solid shapes in the picture. Color them using the key.

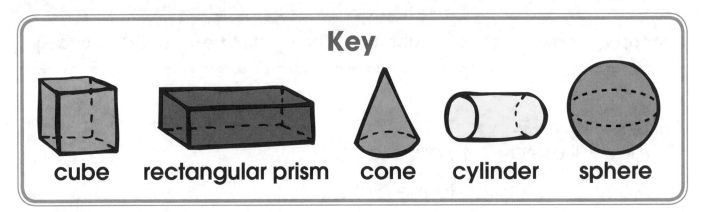

Key

cube   rectangular prism   cone   cylinder   sphere

Color the **telling sentences** yellow. Color the **asking sentences** red. Color the **exclamations blue**. Color the **commands** gray.

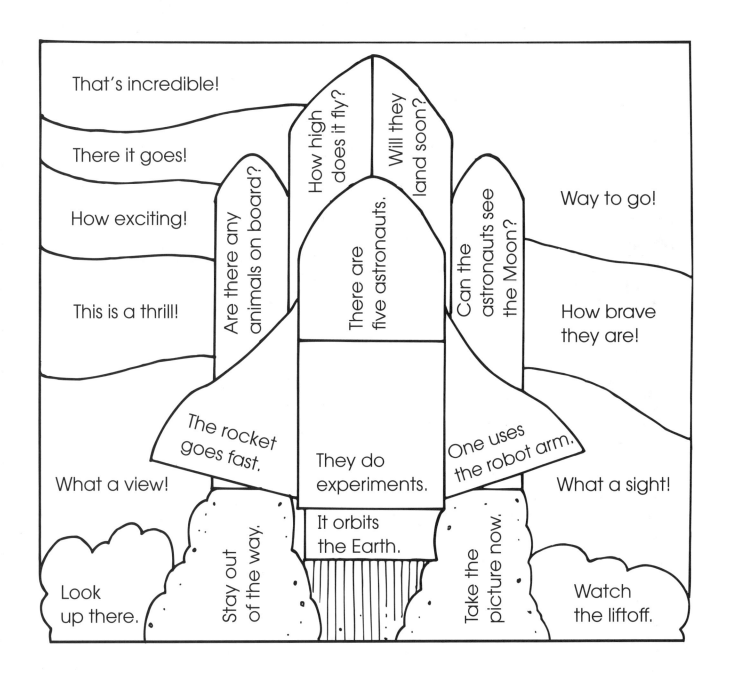

That's incredible!

There it goes!

How exciting!

This is a thrill!

How high does it fly?

Will they land soon?

Are there any animals on board?

There are five astronauts.

Can the astronauts see the Moon?

Way to go!

How brave they are!

The rocket goes fast.

They do experiments.

One uses the robot arm.

What a view!

What a sight!

Stay out of the way.

It orbits the Earth.

Take the picture now.

Look up there.

Watch the liftoff.

Write each word under a category.

baby	donkey	whale	family	fox
uncle	goose	grandfather	kangaroo	policeman

People   ### Animals

Trace the shapes. Then, put them together to draw a new shape.

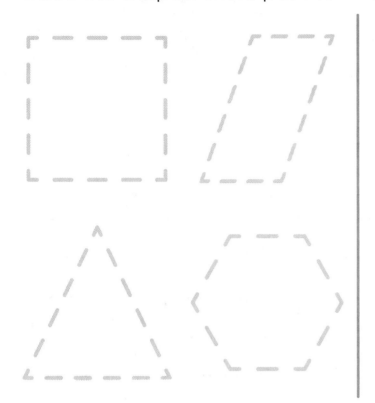

Write **>** or **<** in the circle to show which number in each pair is **greater**. Make sure the "open mouth" points to the larger number.

53 ◯ 76   68 ◯ 80

29 ◯ 26   45 ◯ 19

Color the boxes to show how many bananas were eaten by the monkey.

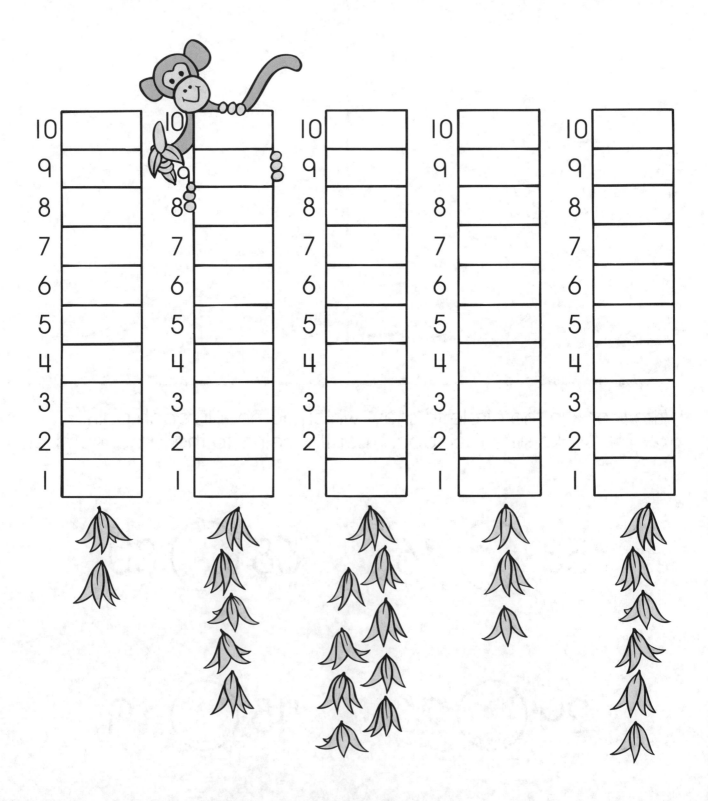

think	tooth	each	thing	change
child	both	inch	teach	thank

1. Write the words that begin like **cheese**.

_____ _____

_____ _____

2. Write the words that begin like **thumb**.

_____ _____ _____

_____ _____ _____

3. Write the words that end like **branch**.

_____ _____ _____

_____ _____ _____

4. Write the words that end like **teeth**.

_____ _____

_____ _____

Write an **end mark** for each sentence.

1. Joey got a huge hit ☐

2. Run to first base ☐

3. Will he make it in time ☐

4. Pete is the next batter ☐

In each pair, circle the number that is **greater**.

| 11 21 | 49 94 | 18 87 |

In each pair, draw an X through the number that is **less**.

| 0 50 | 97 99 | 21 12 |

Write a word to complete each sentence.

| brush | fish | wash |

1. Don't forget to _____ your hands before lunch.

2. Father dropped the _____ into the paint.

3. I have a pet _____.

Write **T** beside the **telling sentence**. Write **A** beside the **asking sentence**. Write **E** beside the **exclamation**. Write **C** beside the **command**.

_____ Two different kinds of penguins live in Antarctica.

_____ Do emperor penguins have black and white bodies?

_____ Look at their webbed feet.

_____ They are amazing!

Write the number that makes each equation true.

$$\begin{array}{r} 20 \\ -\ \Box \\ \hline 4 \end{array} \qquad \begin{array}{r} \Box \\ +\ 8 \\ \hline 15 \end{array} \qquad \begin{array}{r} 7 \\ -\ \Box \\ \hline 7 \end{array} \qquad \begin{array}{r} 5 \\ +\ 11 \\ \hline \Box \end{array}$$

$$\begin{array}{r} 15 \\ -\ \Box \\ \hline 9 \end{array} \qquad \begin{array}{r} \Box \\ +\ 10 \\ \hline 20 \end{array} \qquad \begin{array}{r} \Box \\ -\ 11 \\ \hline 4 \end{array} \qquad \begin{array}{r} 17 \\ +\ 2 \\ \hline \Box \end{array}$$

Write sentences about the picture.

Telling sentence:

- -

Asking sentence:

- -

Exclamation:

- -

Command:

- -

Subtract. Cross out **tens** to help you. The first one is done for you.

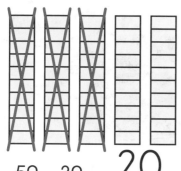

50 – 30 = __20__

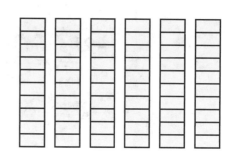

60 – 50 = _____

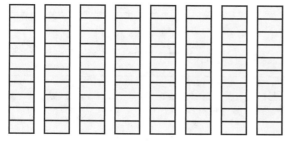

80 – 20 = _____

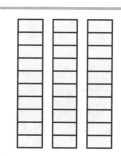

30 – 20 = _____

Write the circled numbers in the correct order on the lines.

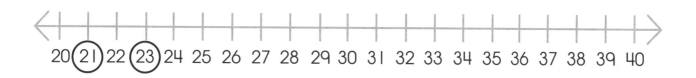

_____ > _____

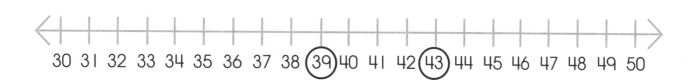

_____ > _____

Write the words in ABC order.

1. _____   5. _____

2. _____   6. _____

3. _____   7. _____

4. _____   8. _____

Say each word. Clap for each **syllable** you hear. Write **1** or **2** on the line to show the number of syllables.

dog _____   timber _____

bedroom _____   cat _____

slipper _____   street _____

Write the missing numbers on the clock face.

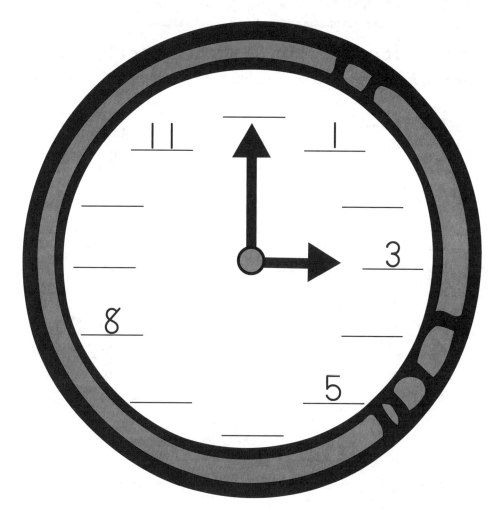

Write the number that is 10 **more**. The first one is done for you.

60, _70_   30, _____

10, _____   50, _____

70, _____   90, _____

Write two words to describe each picture.

rock	shut	road	talk	street	speak	stone	closed

_____

- - - - - - - - - - - - - - - -

_____

- - - - - - - - - - - - - - - -

_____

- - - - - - - - - - - - - - - -

_____

- - - - - - - - - - - - - - - -

_____

- - - - - - - - - - - - - - - -

_____

- - - - - - - - - - - - - - - -

_____

- - - - - - - - - - - - - - - -

_____

- - - - - - - - - - - - - - - -

Write the number that is 10 **less**. The first one is done for you.

<u>70</u> ,80   _____ ,20

_____ ,30   _____ ,50

_____ ,90   _____ ,100

Write each word where it belongs.

car	wind	cake	truck	thunder
candy	bicycle	rain	pie	

1. These things taste sweet.

_____ _____ _____

_ _ _ _ _ _ _ _ _ _ _ _ _ _   _ _ _ _ _ _ _ _ _ _ _ _ _ _   _ _ _ _ _ _ _ _ _ _ _ _ _ _

_____ _____ _____

2. These things come when it storms.

_____ _____ _____

_ _ _ _ _ _ _ _ _ _ _ _ _ _   _ _ _ _ _ _ _ _ _ _ _ _ _ _   _ _ _ _ _ _ _ _ _ _ _ _ _ _

_____ _____ _____

3. These things have wheels.

_____ _____ _____

_ _ _ _ _ _ _ _ _ _ _ _ _ _   _ _ _ _ _ _ _ _ _ _ _ _ _ _   _ _ _ _ _ _ _ _ _ _ _ _ _ _

_____ _____ _____

Write **1**, **2**, and **3** under the boxes to show the order of the story.

_____ _____ _____

Subtract. Cross out **tens** to help you. The first one is done for you.

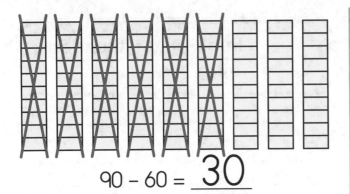

90 – 60 = __30__

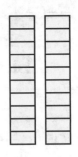

20 – 20 = _____

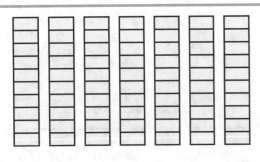

70 – 40 = _____

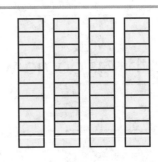

40 – 10 = _____

Write a number to show how many dots in all.

_____ dots

Draw a line to connect two parts of each sentence. Write an **end mark** in the box.

1. Cole is holding up his   great ☐

2. Are you enjoying that   hand ☐

3. I think your drawing is   book ☐

Say each word. Clap for each **syllable** you hear. Write **1** or **2** on the line to show the number of syllables.

tree _____   chalk _____

batter _____   blanket _____

chair _____   marker _____

Write an **adjective**, or describing word, in each blank. Draw a picture to match the sentence.

We saw _____ fish in

the _____ aquarium.

Her _____ car was

parked by the _____ van.

Write the numbers that are 10 **more** and 10 **less**. The first one is done for you.

__10__ , 20, __30__   _____ , 60, _____

_____ , 50, _____   _____ , 90, _____

_____ , 70, _____   _____ , 10, _____

Rewrite the sentences. Begin each one with an uppercase letter. Do not forget to write an **end mark** for each one.

1. is this dog friendly

2. look at the red bird

3. my snake is three feet long

4. oh, no, the cat is going to fall

1. _____

2. _____

3. _____

4. _____

A **noun** that ends with an **apostrophe** (') and **s** shows who or what owns something. For each sentence, circle the correct word to show ownership.

This is _____ coat.

Bettys   Betty's   Betty

I know _____ brother.

Burt's   Burt   Burts

That is the _____ ball.

kitten's   kitten   kittens

My _____ shoe is missing.

sisters   sister   sister's

Write the circled numbers in the correct order on the lines.

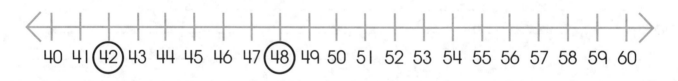

40 41 (42) 43 44 45 46 47 (48) 49 50 51 52 53 54 55 56 57 58 59 60

_____ > _____

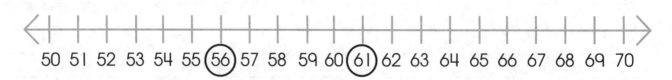

50 51 52 53 54 55 (56) 57 58 59 60 (61) 62 63 64 65 66 67 68 69 70

_____ < _____

Look at the first picture in the row. Circle the picture that shows the **opposite**.

up down over across

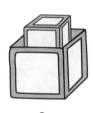  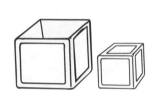 

in beside out over

Subtract.

100 – 0 = _____   100 – 10 = _____   100 – 20 = _____

100 – 30 = _____   100 – 40 = _____   100 – 50 = _____

100 – 60 = _____   100 – 70 = _____   100 – 80 = _____

100 – 90 = _____   100 – 100 = _____

Write each word in the column that matches the spelling of the **r** sound.

| curl | turn | bird | fern | girl | dirt | her | church |

er words	**ir words**	**ur words**

Color to complete the patterns.

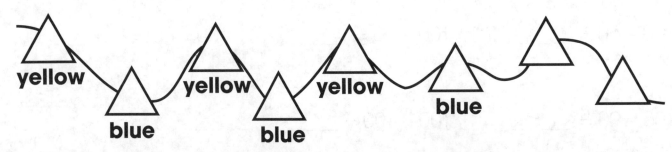

red   blue   blue   red   blue   blue

yellow   blue   yellow   blue   yellow   blue

Draw a line to connect two parts of each sentence. Write an **end mark** in the box.

1. What color is your new   airplane ☐

2. I cannot wait to fly in an   ☐ of toys

3. My brother's train is full   bike ☐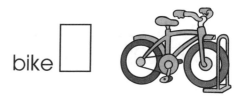

Write the number that is 10 **more**.

20, _____   60, _____

90, _____   80, _____

40, _____   50, _____

A **noun** that ends with **'s** shows ownership. Circle the correct noun to complete each sentence.

1. The doll belongs to Sara.

   It is _____ doll.
         Sara's   Sara

2. Sparky has a red collar.

   _____ collar is red.
     Sparky   Sparky's

3. Jamal has a blue coat.

   _____ coat is blue.
     Jamal's   Jamal

Write the number that is 10 **less**.

_____ , 20   _____ , 60

_____ , 90   _____ , 80

_____ , 40   _____ , 50

Divide each word into two **syllables**. The first one is done for you.

kitten   kit ten   harder _____

lumber _____   dirty _____

winter _____   sister _____

Draw the hands on each clock.

2:30

7:30

11:00

Write the words that **rhyme** with the picture names.

| thorn | born | pork | north | sport | porch | stork |

_____ _____
- - - - - - - - - - - - - - - - - - - - - - - - - -
_____ _____

_____ _____
- - - - - - - - - - - - - - - - - - - - - - - - - -
_____ _____

_____
- - - - - - - - - - - - -
_____

Add.

$$30 + 40$$ $$20 + 10$$ $$50 + 50$$ $$20 + 60$$

$$70 + 20$$ $$10 + 60$$ $$20 + 40$$ $$30 + 30$$

When you write a sentence to tell what will happen in the future, use **will** before the **verb**. Rewrite each sentence with a **future-tense verb**. The first one is done for you.

1. She dives in the pool.

   She will dive in the pool.

2. Dad hiked on Saturday.

   -

3. Ruff needs to go to the vet.

   -

Draw a shape to complete each pattern.

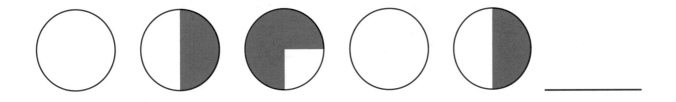

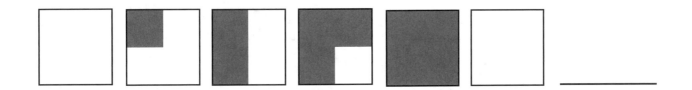

Circle the correct word to complete each sentence.

1. The _____ lunch box is broken.   boy's   boys

2. _____ hair is brown.   Anns   Ann's

3. The _____ fur is black.   cat's   cats

4. The _____ paws are muddy.   dogs   dog's

Subtract.

$$100 - 40$$ $$40 - 10$$ $$70 - 60$$ $$80 - 50$$

$$90 - 40$$ $$100 - 20$$ $$70 - 20$$ $$30 - 30$$

Write the words in ABC order.

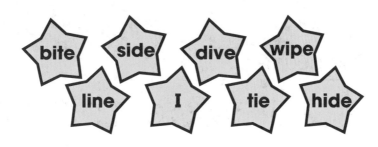

1. _____

2. _____

3. _____

4. _____

5. _____

6. _____

7. _____

8. _____

Write **>** or **<** in the circle to show which number in each pair is **greater**. Make sure the "open mouth" points to the larger number.

90 ◯ 89   70 ◯ 67

46 ◯ 86   22 ◯ 12

Rewrite each sentence with a **future-tense verb**. The first one is done for you.

1. Marty wiped the counter.

    Marty will wipe the counter.

2. Suki helps wash the car.

    _____

    -

    _____

3. The lady painted my face.

    _____

    -

    _____

Write the time shown on each clock.

___ : ___   ___ : ___   ___ : ___

Circle the word that is spelled correctly. Write it on the line.

touch
tuch
touh

- - - - - - - - - - - - - - - - - - - -

smel
smll
smell

- - - - - - - - - - - - - - - - - - - -

her
hear
har

- - - - - - - - - - - - - - - - - - - -

Add the **tens** and **ones**. Write the sum. The first one is done for you.

2 tens and **6 ones**	**1 ten** and **4 ones**
+ **1 ten** and **0 ones**	+ **3 tens** and **0 ones**

_3_ **tens** and _6_ **ones** = _36_   ___ tens and ___ ones = _____

7 tens and **3 ones**	**1 ten** and **6 ones**
+ **2 tens** and **0 ones**	+ **3 tens** and **0 ones**

___ tens and ___ ones = _____   ___ tens and ___ ones = _____

Circle the correct word to complete each sentence.

1. The _____ cage needs to
   be cleaned.   gerbils   gerbil's

2. My _____ coat is torn.   sister's   sister

3. The _____ neck is long.   giraffes   giraffe's

4. The _____ paws are big
   and powerful.   lion's   lions

Color the boxes to show how many spots are on each turtle's shell.

1	2	3	4	5	6	7	8

1	2	3	4	5	6	7	8

1	2	3	4	5	6	7	8

Choose the word that describes the picture. Write it on the line.

1. sew   so

2. pair   pear

3. eye   I

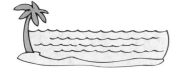

4. see   sea

Write the number that is 10 **more**. The first one is done for you.

21, __31__   54, _____

56, _____   13, _____

83, _____   65, _____

If the words have **opposite** meanings, color the space orange. If the words have the **same** meanings, color the space blue.

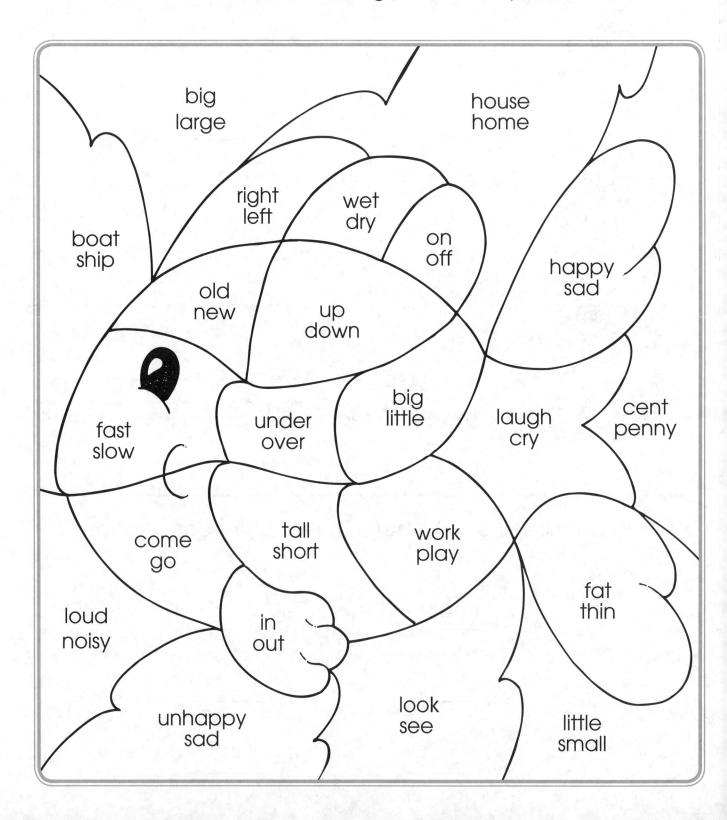

Some **pronouns** can stand for any person, place, or thing. Write a word from the box to finish each sentence.

| someone | anybody | anything |

1. Has _____ noticed the rain?

2. Will _____ check the backyard?

3. Is _____ out there that cannot get wet?

Add the **tens** and **ones**. Write the sum.

   1 ten   and   **3 ones**
+ **1 ten**   and   **0 ones**

___ **tens** and ___ **ones** = _____

   2 tens and   **5 ones**
+ **2 tens** and   **0 ones**

___ **tens** and ___ **ones** = _____

   1 ten   and   **5 ones**
+ **2 tens** and   **0 ones**

___ **tens** and ___ **ones** = _____

   2 tens and   **3 ones**
+ **2 tens** and   **0 ones**

___ **tens** and ___ **ones** = _____

Add **'s** to the bold **noun** in the first sentence. Write the new word to complete the second sentence.

1. The tail of the **cat** is short.

_____

The _____ tail is short.

2. The name of my **mother** is Karen.

_____

My _____ name is Karen.

3. The nest of the **bird** is finished.

_____

The _____ nest is finished.

Write the number that is 10 **less**. The first one is done for you.

__5__ , 15   _____ , 73

_____ , 22   _____ , 44

_____ , 99   _____ , 18

Write each word where it belongs.

Stop	**bush**	**rocket**	**Danger**	**grass**
airplane	**Poison**	**flower**	**bird**	

1. These are words you see on signs.

_____ _____ _____
- - - - - - - - - - - - - - - - - - - - - - - - - - -
_____ _____ _____

2. These things can fly.

_____ _____ _____
- - - - - - - - - - - - - - - - - - - - - - - - - - -
_____ _____ _____

3. These things grow in the ground.

_____ _____ _____
- - - - - - - - - - - - - - - - - - - - - - - - - - -
_____ _____ _____

Color the bowls in each row to show how many fish.

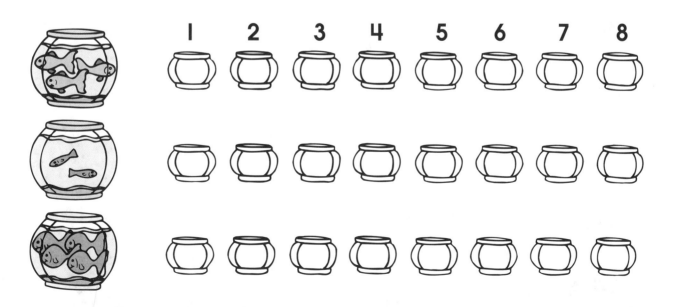

When a word has double consonants, divide it between the consonants. Divide each word into two **syllables**. The first one is done for you.

| butter | dinner | pillow | puppy | chatter | letter |

but ter

Match the number to the word.

two   1

four   9

seven   2

three   3

one   4

nine   7

Write a **pronoun** from the box to finish each sentence.

> each   many   anyone

1. Has _____ seen some lost sheep?

2. _____ are missing from the barn.

3. _____ one belongs back at home.

Add the numbers in the **ones** column. Then, add the numbers in the **tens** column. The first one is done for you.

tens	ones
2	5
+1	0
3	5

tens	ones
5	3
+3	0

tens	ones
7	1
+2	0

tens	ones
4	4
+3	0

tens	ones
5	1
+3	0

tens	ones
2	6
+5	0

Draw an X on the word in each row that does not belong.

1.   flashlight   candle   radio   fire

2.   shirt   pants   coat   bat

3.   cow   car   bus   train

4.   beans   hot dog   ball   bread

Write the numbers that are 10 **more** and 10 **less**. The first one is done for you.

__53__ , 63, __73__   _____ , 84, _____

_____ , 19, _____   _____ , 28, _____

_____ , 55, _____   _____ , 79, _____

For each sentence, circle the correct word to show ownership.

The _____ nose is big.

clown   clowns   clown's

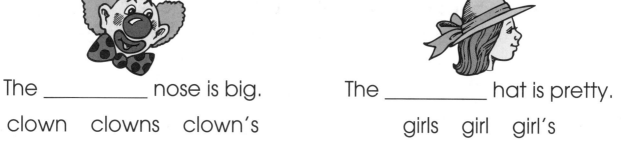

The _____ hat is pretty.

girls   girl   girl's

The _____ coach is Mr. Hall.

team   team's   teams

The _____ cover is torn.

book's   books   book

Draw the hands on the sock clocks.

10:00

3:30

9:30

Choose a **verb** to complete each sentence.

bakes   will bake   baked

1. Yesterday, Panda _____ cookies.

2. Today, Panda _____ more cookies.

3. Tomorrow, Panda _____ even more cookies!

Draw the shape that comes next in each pattern.

Write a number to show each group of **tens**. Then, **add** to find the sum. The first one is done for you.

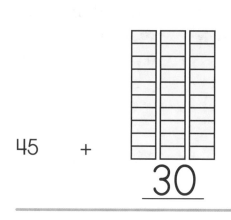

45   +   = <u>75</u>

<u>30</u>

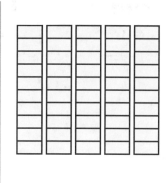

+ 22 = _____

_____

72   +   = _____

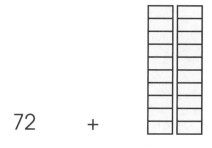

_____

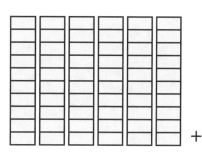

+ 34 = _____

_____

Divide each word into two **syllables**. The first one is done for you.

winter      little

funny   _____   dinner   _____

pencil   _____   mailbox   _____

Add. Use number words to complete the puzzle.

one	three	five	seven	nine
two	four	six	eight	ten

Across

1. 3 + 2 = _____

2. 4 + 2 = _____

3. 2 + 1 = _____

4. 1 + 0 = _____

5. 5 + 3 = _____

7. 2 + 7 = _____

Down

1. 2 + 2 = _____

2. 4 + 3 = _____

3. 0 + 2 = _____

6. 4 + 6 = _____

Write **PR** in front of sentences with **present-tense verbs**. Write **PA** in front of sentences with **past-tense verbs**. Write **F** in front of sentences with **future-tense verbs**.

_____ The friends play checkers.

_____ They also played yesterday.

_____ They will play two games on Monday.

_____ They will play again on Tuesday.

_____ They play almost every day.

_____ Once, they played until dark.

Circle the word in each row that is most like the first word.

grin	smile	frown	mad
bag	jar	sack	box
cat	fruit	kitten	flower
apple	rot	cookie	orange

Write a **pronoun** from the box to finish each sentence.

| others | everybody | some |

1. Did _____ enjoy the pizzas?

2. _____ had peppers and pineapples.

3. _____ had mushrooms and tomatoes.

Add the numbers in the **ones** column. Then, add the numbers in the **tens** column.

tens	ones
2	6
+4	0

tens	ones
3	7
+5	0

tens	ones
1	9
+3	0

tens	ones
6	5
+3	0

tens	ones
1	8
+8	0

tens	ones
5	7
+1	0

Choose a word to complete each sentence. Write it on the line.

1. This is a present _____ your birthday.
   four   for

2. We _____ in the car for two hours.
   road   rode

3. The boys will either swim _____ go to the ball
   game.   oar   or

4. The scrape on his knee caused a lot of _____.
                                          pane   pain

Write the number that is 10 **more**.

52, _____   29, _____

88, _____   41, _____

16, _____   76, _____

Fill in the missing letters to spell each word twice.

tr _ _  _ _ ee

gr _ ss  _ a _ _

s _ nd  _ a _ _

Write the missing numbers.

102, _____ , _____ , _____ , _____ , _____ , _____ , 109,

_____ , _____ , _____ , _____ , _____ , _____ , 116, _____ ,

_____ , 119, _____

Rewrite each sentence. Change the **verb** to the **verb tense** shown.

1. The boys race each other. (future)

   _____

   -

   _____

2. They lined up. (present)

   _____

   -

   _____

3. The race starts. (past)

   _____

   -

   _____

Write the number that is 10 **less**.

_____ , 93   _____ , 51

_____ , 16   _____ , 28

_____ , 77   _____ , 89

Write a **noun** in each chart. Then, write an **adjective**, or describing word, to answer each question.

Noun	What Color?	What Size?	What Number?

Noun	What Color?	What Size?	What Number?

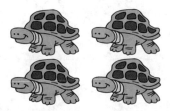

Count the objects and write the number word.

  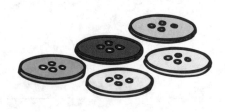

_____   _____   _____

Write a number to show each group of **tens**. Then, **add** to find the sum.

66 + 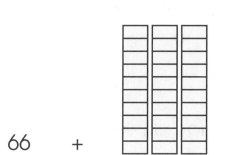 = _____

_____

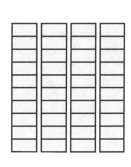 + 17 = _____

_____

43 + 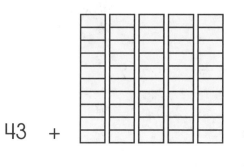 = _____

_____

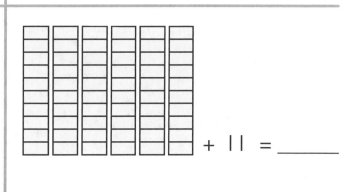 + 11 = _____

_____

Draw lines to connect the words that are **opposites**.

up   wet

over   down

dry   dirty

clean   under

Write a word from the box to complete each sentence.

drank	sipped	gulped

1. The little girl _____ the strange drink.

2. I _____ milk for lunch.

3. The boy was so thirsty that he _____ the water.

Add.

11 + 10 = _____   11 + 20 = _____

11 + 30 = _____   11 + 40 = _____

11 + 50 = _____   11 + 60 = _____

11 + 70 = _____   11 + 80 = _____

Draw an X on the word in each row that does not belong.

1.	gloves		hat		book		boots

2.	fork		butter		cup		plate

3.	book		ball		bat		milk

4.	dogs		bees		flies		ants

Look at the shapes. Divide and color the blank shapes in the same way.

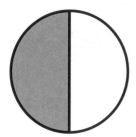 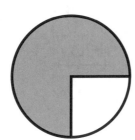 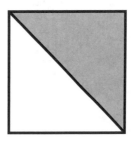 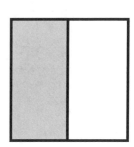

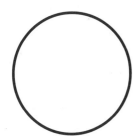 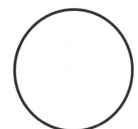 

Write the words in ABC order. The first one is done for you.

| bath | bang | teeth | rang | path | hang | math | sang |

1. bang

2. _____

3. _____

4. _____

5. _____

6. _____

7. _____

8. _____

Add.

$$30 + 66$$

$$58 + 10$$

$$40 + 37$$

$$51 + 40$$

$$20 + 62$$

$$12 + 80$$

$$30 + 19$$

$$66 + 20$$

Write a word from the box to complete each sentence.

| large | tiny | gigantic |

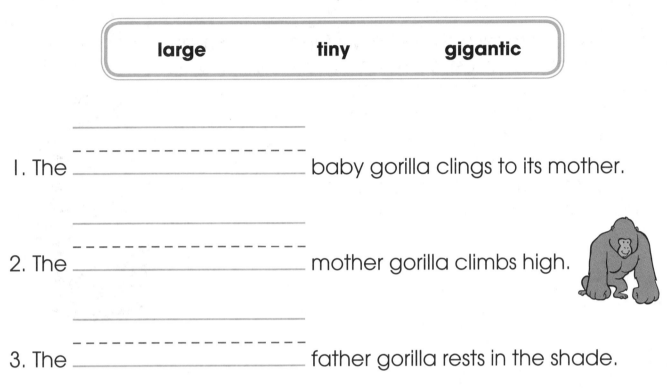

1. The _____ baby gorilla clings to its mother.

2. The _____ mother gorilla climbs high.

3. The _____ father gorilla rests in the shade.

Stars shrink as they get older. As they shrink, they change colors. Use the key to color the stars.

Key

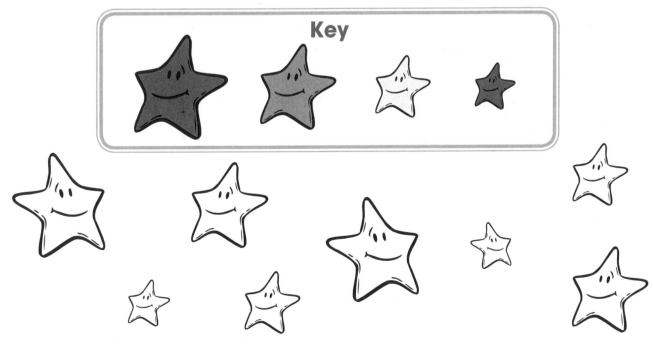

Read the passage. Answer the questions.

    Here is how to play Simon Says: One kid is Simon. Simon is the leader. Everyone must do what Simon says and does but only if the leader says, "Simon says" first. Let's try it. "Simon says, 'Pat your head.'" "Simon says, 'Pat your nose. Pat your toes.'" Oops! Did you pat your toes? I did not say, "Simon says" first. If you patted your toes, you are out!

1. Who is the leader in this game?

    _____

    _____

2. What must the leader say first each time?

    _____

    _____

3. What happens if you do something and the leader did not say, "Simon says"?

    _____

    _____

Draw a line from each shape to an object with the same shape.

 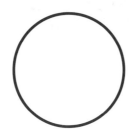  

Add.

$$\begin{array}{r} 80 \\ + 13 \\ \hline \end{array} \qquad \begin{array}{r} 71 \\ + 10 \\ \hline \end{array} \qquad \begin{array}{r} 50 \\ + 27 \\ \hline \end{array} \qquad \begin{array}{r} 69 \\ + 30 \\ \hline \end{array}$$

$$\begin{array}{r} 50 \\ + 15 \\ \hline \end{array} \qquad \begin{array}{r} 64 \\ + 10 \\ \hline \end{array} \qquad \begin{array}{r} 80 \\ + 11 \\ \hline \end{array} \qquad \begin{array}{r} 39 \\ + 20 \\ \hline \end{array}$$

A **prefix** is added to the beginning of a **root word**. It changes the word's meaning. Add the prefixes to the root words to write new words.

1.   re   +   do =   _____
     (again)   (do again)

2.   un   +   tie =   _____
   (opposite of)   (opposite of tie)

3.   pre   +   game = _____
    (before)   (before the game)

4.   dis   +   obey = _____
     (not)   (not obey)

Copy the picture. How many different shapes did you use?

Find two words with **opposite** meanings in each sentence. Write them in the boxes.

1. I thought I lost my dog, but someone found him.

[ ] [ ]

2. The teacher will ask questions for the students to answer.

[ ] [ ]

3. Airplanes arrive and depart at the airport.

[ ] [ ]

Add or **subtract**.

$$\begin{array}{r} 70 \\ +\ 12 \\ \hline \end{array}$$ $$\begin{array}{r} 90 \\ -\ 60 \\ \hline \end{array}$$ $$\begin{array}{r} 50 \\ +\ 32 \\ \hline \end{array}$$ $$\begin{array}{r} 40 \\ -\ 20 \\ \hline \end{array}$$

$$\begin{array}{r} 80 \\ +\ 19 \\ \hline \end{array}$$ $$\begin{array}{r} 60 \\ -\ 50 \\ \hline \end{array}$$ $$\begin{array}{r} 20 \\ +\ 77 \\ \hline \end{array}$$ $$\begin{array}{r} 70 \\ -\ 30 \\ \hline \end{array}$$

Name_____

Combine each pair of sentences into one sentence using the word **and**. The first one is done for you.

1. Holly is jumping rope. Molly is jumping rope.

Holly and Molly are jumping rope.

2. A frog swims in the water. A fish swims in the water.

- -

- -

In each sentence, circle two words that sound the same, but have different spellings and meanings.

1. Tom ate eight grapes.

2. Five blue feathers blew in the wind.

3. Would you get wood for the fire?

Add the blocks. Write the sum. The first one is done for you.

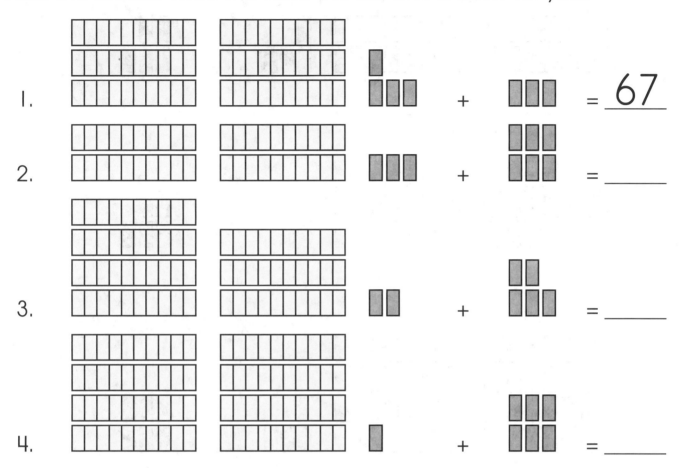

1. = 67

2. =

3. =

4. =

Circle the shapes divided into equal parts. Draw an X on shapes divided into unequal parts.

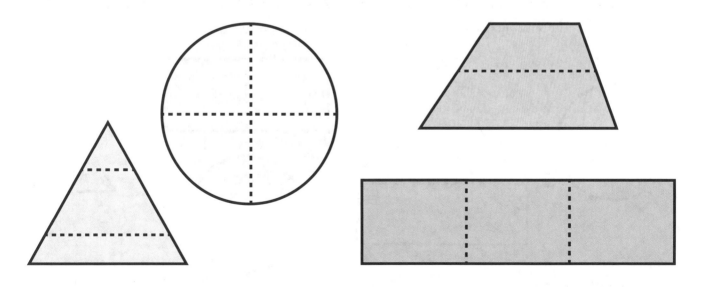

Write the numbers shown by the blocks. **Add** to find the sum.

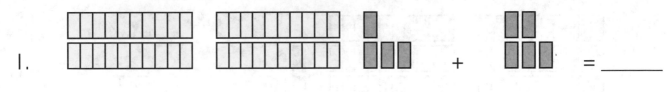

1. _____ + _____ = _____

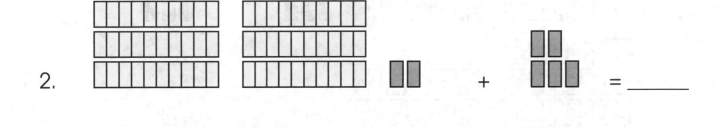

2. _____ + _____ = _____

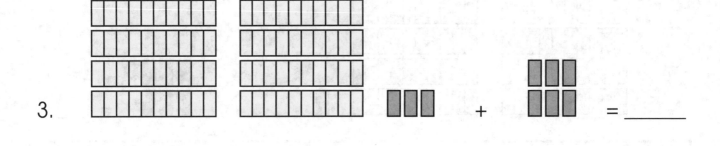

3. _____ + _____ = _____

When a shape is divided into **halves**, it has **two** equal parts. Color the shapes that show halves.

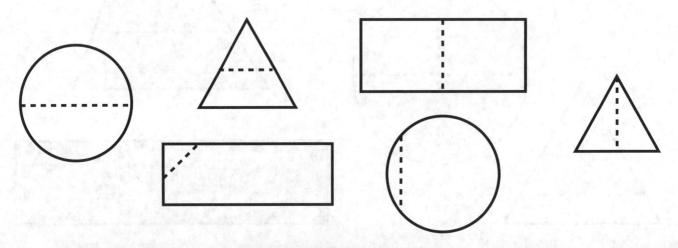

Commas are used to separate words in a series of three or more. Look at the commas in this sentence:

I like apples**,** bananas**,** and oranges.

Write commas where they are needed in the sentences.

1. Please buy milk eggs bread and cheese.

2. I need a folder paper and pencils for school.

Circle the word in each row that is most like the first word.

around	**circle**	**square**	**dot**
brown	**tan**	**black**	**red**
bird	**dog**	**cat**	**duck**
bee	**fish**	**ant**	**snake**

Add a **prefix** to the **root word** in each sentence.

un	mis	dis	im

1. Do you _____ agree with me?

2. I found a _____ take.

3. This puzzle is _____ possible!

4. The _____ happy toddler screamed.

Add the **ones**. Then, add the **tens**.

tens	ones
3	3
+	5

tens	ones
7	4
+	4

tens	ones
8	4
+	2

tens	ones
7	5
+	4

tens	ones
1	2
+	6

tens	ones
5	5
+	1

Combine each pair of sentences into one sentence using the word **and**. The first one is done for you.

1. The truck has wheels. The bike has wheels.

The truck and bike have wheels.

2. Rosa has a ticket. I have a ticket.

_____

- -

_____

- -

Look at the shapes. Divide and color the blank shapes in the same way.

  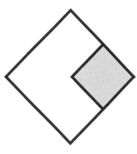 

  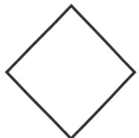 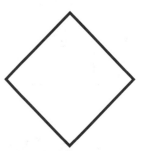

Complete the chart.

Prefix	Root Word	New Word
dis	like	
un		undone
	pay	prepay
in	active	
mis	take	

Add the **ones**. Then, add the **tens**.

tens	ones
1	0
+	9

tens	ones
2	8
+	1

tens	ones
6	7
+	2

tens	ones
3	2
+	7

tens	ones
6	6
+	3

tens	ones
7	2
+	7

Write **commas** where they are needed in the sentences.

1. Some good pets are cats dogs gerbils fish and rabbits.

2. Aaron Mike and Matt went to the baseball game.

3. Major forms of transportation are planes trains and automobiles.

 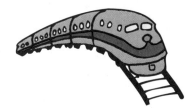 

When a shape is divided into **halves**, it has **two** equal parts. Color the shapes that show halves.

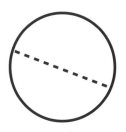 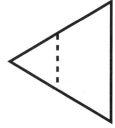 

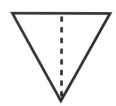  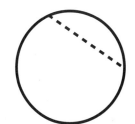

Divide each word into two **syllables** between two consonant letters. The first one is done for you.

window	mister	barber	doctor	winter	sister

win dow

Color one **half** of each shape.

Combine each pair of sentences into one sentence using the word **and**. The first one is done for you.

1. Tom can jump. Tom can run.

Tom can run and jump.

2. The dog can roll over. The dog can bark.

Add.

$$\begin{array}{r} 56 \\ + 3 \\ \hline \end{array} \qquad \begin{array}{r} 81 \\ + 8 \\ \hline \end{array} \qquad \begin{array}{r} 36 \\ + 3 \\ \hline \end{array} \qquad \begin{array}{r} 15 \\ + 4 \\ \hline \end{array}$$

$$\begin{array}{r} 25 \\ + 2 \\ \hline \end{array} \qquad \begin{array}{r} 46 \\ + 2 \\ \hline \end{array} \qquad \begin{array}{r} 81 \\ + 7 \\ \hline \end{array} \qquad \begin{array}{r} 12 \\ + 6 \\ \hline \end{array}$$

Add the blocks. Write the sum. The first one is done for you.

1. 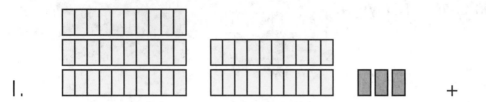 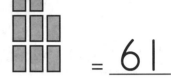 = $\underline{61}$

2. = _____

3. = _____

4. = _____

Divide each picture into equal **halves**. Color the pictures.

| back | call | king | pick | key | cake |

1. Write the words beginning with **c** that makes the **k** sound.

_____   _____

_____   _____

2. Write the words beginning with **k** that makes the **k** sound.

_____   _____

_____   _____

3. Write the words ending with **ck** that makes the **k** sound.

_____   _____

_____   _____

Have you ever seen a falling star? Falling stars are not really stars. They are small pieces of rock. As falling stars fall, they get hot and burn. They look big because they give off so much light. That is why they are so bright in the night sky. Did you know that **meteor** is another name for a falling star?

Circle the correct answer.

A falling star is really a star.   **Yes**   **No**

Falling stars are pieces of rock.   **Yes**   **No**

Falling stars burn as they fall.   **Yes**   **No**

Combine each pair of sentences into one sentence using the word **and**. The first one is done for you.

1. Mom plays with me. Mom reads with me.

Mom plays and reads with me.

2. Tara is tall. Tara is smart.

_____

- -

_____

- -

_____

Look at each word in **bold**. Circle the **prefix**. Write the root word on the line.

1. The **preview** of the movie was funny.

2. We always drink **nonfat** milk.

3. I have **outgrown** my new shoes already.

4. You must have **misplaced** the papers.

Write the numbers shown by the blocks. **Add** to find the sum.

1. 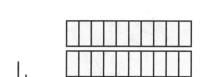 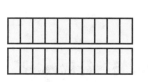 +  = _____

   _____   _____

2. 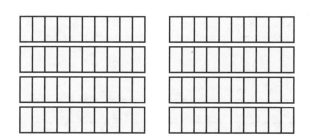 + 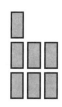 = _____

   _____   _____

3.   + = _____

      +

   _____   _____

Connect the dots to draw one shape with four sides and one shape with three sides.

• • • • • • • • • •

• • • • • • • • • •

• • • • • • • • • •

• • • • • • • • • •

Write an invitation for a party to celebrate your birthday. The party should last for three hours.

 **You are invited!**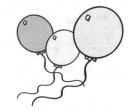

_____

Where: _____

Date: _____

Time It Begins: _____

Time It Ends: _____

Write **>** or **<** in the circle to show which number in each pair is **greater**. Make sure the "open mouth" points to the larger number.

11 ◯ 100   18 ◯ 48

52 ◯ 25   77 ◯ 27

When the sum of the **ones** is more than 10, **regroup** the **tens**. Look at the examples. Trace the numbers.

Step 1: Add the ones.   **Step 2:** Regroup the tens.   **Step 3:** Add the tens.

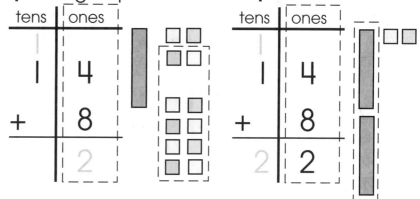

tens	ones
1	4
+	8
	12

tens	ones
1	4
+	8
	2

tens	ones
1	4
+	8
2	2

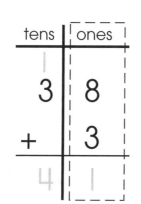

tens	ones
1	6
+	7
2	3

tens	ones
3	8
+	3
4	1

tens	ones
2	4
+	7
3	1

---

rain	day	sail	way	wait	say

1. Write the **ai** words that make the **long a** sound.

_____   _____   _____

2. Write the **ay** words that make the **long a** sound.

_____   _____   _____

Combine each pair of sentences into one sentence using the joining word **and**. Write a comma before the joining word. The first one is done for you.

1. **(and)** I took my dog for a walk. I played with my cat.

I took my dog for a walk, and I played with my cat.

2. **(and)** My sister had a birthday. She got a new bike.

_____
- - - - - - - - - - - - - - - - - -
_____
- - - - - - - - - - - - - - - - - -
_____

Look at each word in **bold**. Circle the **prefix**. Write the root word on the line.

1. I **disliked** that book.

_____
- - - - - - - - - - - - - - - - - -
_____

2. Please try to keep the cat **inside** the house.

_____
- - - - - - - - - - - - - - - - - -
_____

3. That song is total **nonsense**!

_____
- - - - - - - - - - - - - - - - - -
_____

4. Can you help me **unzip** this jacket?

_____

Add. Regroup the tens. The first one is done for you.

tens	ones
1	
2	8
+	7
3	5

tens	ones
3	2
+	8

tens	ones
5	4
+	7

tens	ones
1	9
+	5

tens	ones
4	4
+	8

tens	ones
2	5
+	6

When a shape is divided into **fourths** or **quarters**, it has **four** equal parts. Color the shapes that show fourths.

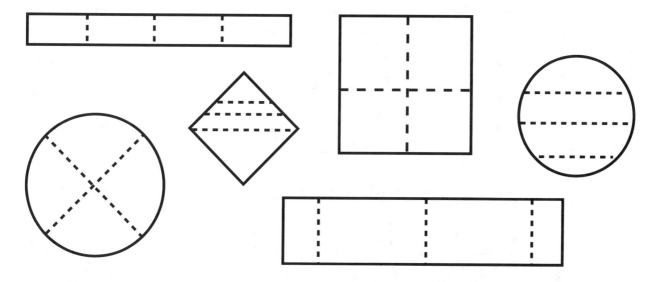

Add. **Regroup** the tens. The first one is done for you.

tens	ones
1 2	9
+	3
3	2

tens	ones
6	6
+	5

tens	ones
7	4
+	7

tens	ones
1	5
+	5

tens	ones
7	2
+	9

tens	ones
3	6
+	8

Color one **fourth** of each shape.

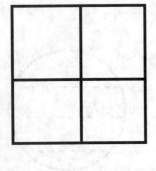

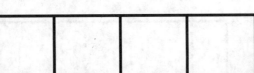
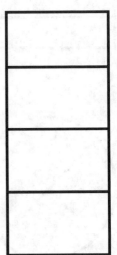

A **suffix** is added to the ending of a **root word**. It changes the word's meaning. Add the suffixes to the root words to write new words.

1. color   +   ful = _____
                         (full of color)

2. care   +   less = _____
                         (without care)

3. work   +   er =   _____
                         (someone who works)

4. climb   +   ed =   _____
                         (did climb)

Babies are small. Some babies cry a lot. They cry when they are wet. They cry when they are hungry. They smile when they are dry. They smile when they are fed.

1. Name two reasons babies cry.

_____   _____

_____   _____

2. Name two reasons babies smile.

_____   _____

_____   _____

Combine each pair of sentences into one sentence using the joining word **or**. Write a comma before the joining word. The first one is done for you.

1. **(or)** You could eat the cookie. You could give it to me.

   ## You could eat the cookie, or you could give it to me.

2. **(or)** We can play outside. We can play inside.

When a shape is divided into **fourths** or **quarters**, it has **four** equal parts. Color the shapes that show fourths.

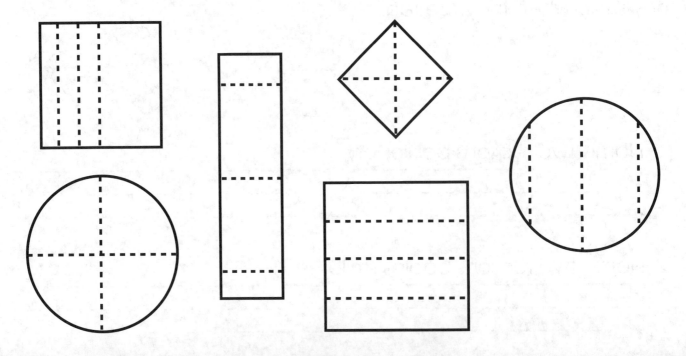

Add. If needed, **regroup** the **tens**.

tens	ones
3	8
+	6

tens	ones
5	4
+	7

tens	ones
4	9
+	3

tens	ones
6	2
+	6

tens	ones
2	6
+	7

tens	ones
1	5
+	4

Write each word under the spelling of its **long e** sound.

baby	seat	party	sheet	happy
feet	weed	read	meat	

ea **ee** **y**

Read the passage. Then, write the steps to grow a flower.

First, find a sunny spot. Then, plant the seed. Water it. The flower will start to grow. Pull the weeds around it. Remember to keep giving the flower water. Enjoy your flower.

1. _____

2. _____

3. _____

4. _____

5. _____

Add. If needed, **regroup** the **tens**.

tens	ones
1	8
+	4

tens	ones
8	5
+	5

tens	ones
8	8
+	3

tens	ones
6	3
+	3

tens	ones
4	1
+	6

tens	ones
6	7
+	4

Divide each picture into equal **fourths**. Color the pictures.

Color the **fourth** ball **orange**.

Color the **sixth** ball **red**.

Add to find the points scored in each game. Add the **ones** first, **regroup**, and then add the **tens**.

HOME 33
VISITOR 7

Total _____

HOME 3
VISITOR 49

Total _____

HOME 7
VISITOR 34

Total _____

HOME 29
VISITOR 2

Total _____

Combine each pair of sentences into one sentence using the joining word **but**. Write a comma before the joining word. The first one is done for you.

1. **(but)**
I want to play outside. It is raining.

I want to play outside, but it is raining.

2. **(but)**
My aunt lives far away. She calls me often.

Complete the chart.

Root Word	Suffix	New Word
	ing	biking
harm	ful	
	es	dishes
walk		walked
art	ist	

Circle the shapes that show **halves**. Draw a box around the shapes that show **fourths**.

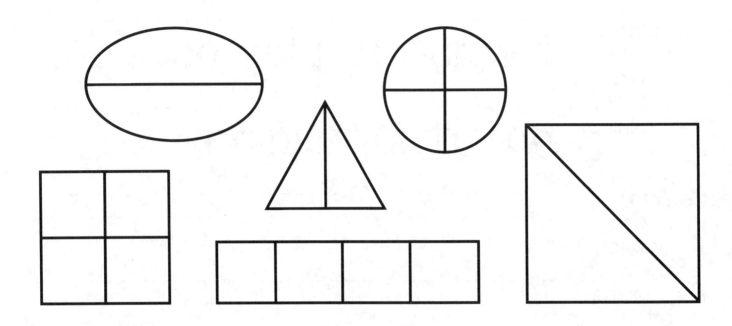

Add. **Regroup** if needed.

$$\begin{array}{r} 36 \\ +\ 6 \\ \hline \end{array}\qquad \begin{array}{r} 75 \\ +\ 7 \\ \hline \end{array}\qquad \begin{array}{r} 55 \\ +\ 3 \\ \hline \end{array}\qquad \begin{array}{r} 61 \\ +\ 9 \\ \hline \end{array}$$

$$\begin{array}{r} 40 \\ +\ 12 \\ \hline \end{array}\qquad \begin{array}{r} 47 \\ +\ 5 \\ \hline \end{array}\qquad \begin{array}{r} 28 \\ +\ 4 \\ \hline \end{array}\qquad \begin{array}{r} 16 \\ +\ 3 \\ \hline \end{array}$$

Add a **suffix** to the **root word** in each sentence.

| or | ing | less | ed |

1. Aunt Sara is cook_____ dinner.

2. This old ticket is worth_____.

3. The ship sail_____ this morning.

4. I want to be an act_____ in the play.

| light | fly | dry | right | by | might |

1. Write the **igh** words that make the **long i** sound.

_____ _____ _____

_____ _____ _____

2. Write the words ending in **y** that make the **long i** sound.

_____ _____ _____

_____ _____ _____

Read the words with **suffixes**. Write each one next to its **root word**.

coming	visited	running	carried	swimming
lived	hurried	rained	sitting	racing

run _____   come _____

live _____   carry _____

hurry _____   race _____

swim _____   rain _____

visit _____   sit _____

Add to find the points scored in each game. Add the **ones** first, **regroup**, and then add the **tens**.

Total _____

Total _____

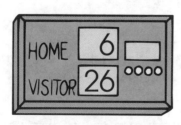

Total _____

Total _____

These shapes show **halves**. Draw a line to divide each shape into **fourths**.

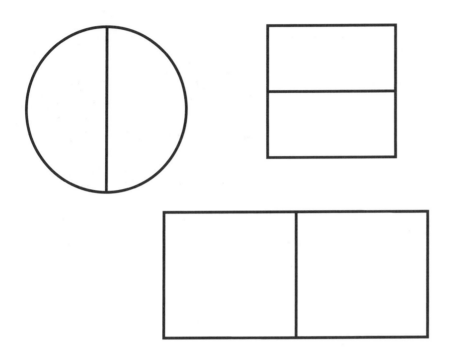

Combine the two sentences into one sentence. Decide which joining word to use: **or, and,** or **but**. Write a comma after the joining word.

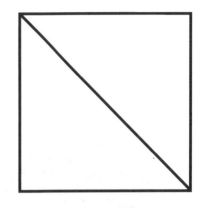

My uncle likes popcorn. He does not like peanuts.

_____

_____

_____

_____

_____

_____

Fluffy, Blackie, and Tiger are playing. Tom is sleeping. Blackie has spots. Tiger has stripes. Write the name of each cat.

1. _____

2. _____

3. _____

4. _____

Add or **subtract**.

$$\begin{array}{r} 90 \\ -60 \\ \hline \end{array} \qquad \begin{array}{r} 12 \\ +\ 7 \\ \hline \end{array} \qquad \begin{array}{r} 48 \\ +\ 6 \\ \hline \end{array} \qquad \begin{array}{r} 59 \\ +30 \\ \hline \end{array}$$

$$\begin{array}{r} 20 \\ -\ 7 \\ \hline \end{array} \qquad \begin{array}{r} 50 \\ -20 \\ \hline \end{array} \qquad \begin{array}{r} 79 \\ +\ 6 \\ \hline \end{array} \qquad \begin{array}{r} 62 \\ +30 \\ \hline \end{array}$$

Color one **half** of each shape.

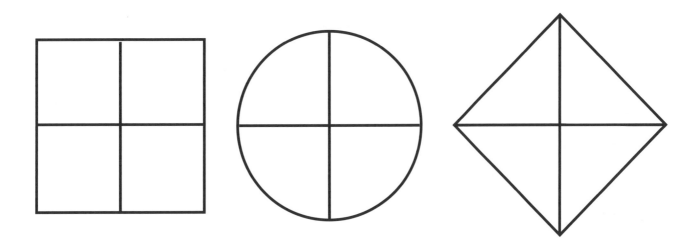

joke   sow   grow   hope   woke   know

1. Write the words ending with **e** that make the **long o** sound.

_____ _____ _____

- - - - - - - - - - - - - - - - - - - - - - - - - - - - - - - - - -

_____ _____ _____

2. Write the **ow** words that make the **long o** sound.

_____ _____ _____

- - - - - - - - - - - - - - - - - - - - - - - - - - - - - - - - - -

_____ _____ _____

Write a **root word** with a **suffix** for each meaning.

blame + less	cheer + ful	rain + y	bump + y

1. full of cheer

2. having bumps

3. without blame

4. having rain

Combine the two sentences into one sentence. Decide which joining word to use: **or, and**, or **but**. Write a comma after the joining word.

He could read a book. He could tell me his own story.

Two **halves** make one **whole**. Four **fourths** make one whole. Circle the shapes that show wholes.

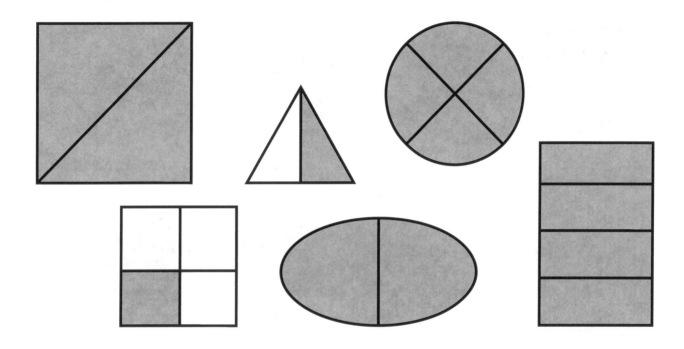

Add or **subtract**.

70	15	75	44
− 20	+ 4	+ 8	+ 40

19	90	28	63
− 6	− 10	+ 6	+ 20

Say the name of the first picture in each row. Circle the pictures that have the same sound.

couch

howl

Add or **subtract**.

$$
\begin{array}{r} 50 \\ -\ 50 \\ \hline \end{array}
\qquad
\begin{array}{r} 8 \\ +\ 11 \\ \hline \end{array}
\qquad
\begin{array}{r} 36 \\ +\ 5 \\ \hline \end{array}
\qquad
\begin{array}{r} 52 \\ +\ 20 \\ \hline \end{array}
$$

$$
\begin{array}{r} 15 \\ -\ 3 \\ \hline \end{array}
\qquad
\begin{array}{r} 100 \\ -\ 60 \\ \hline \end{array}
\qquad
\begin{array}{r} 44 \\ +\ 9 \\ \hline \end{array}
\qquad
\begin{array}{r} 15 \\ +\ 60 \\ \hline \end{array}
$$

Write each word next to its picture.

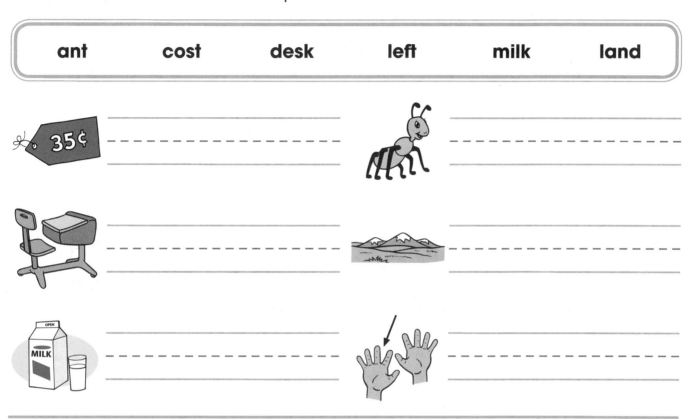

| ant | cost | desk | left | milk | land |

Draw hands on the sock clocks.

1:30

4:00

2:30

Add or **subtract**.

$$60 - 50$$

$$11 + 3$$

$$66 + 6$$

$$71 + 10$$

$$20 - 11$$

$$100 - 50$$

$$58 + 8$$

$$25 + 30$$

Combine the two sentences into one sentence. Decide which joining word to use: **or**, **and**, or **but**. Write a comma after the joining word.

My little brother is sleepy. He wants to go to bed.

_____

- -

_____

- -

_____

- -

In each sentence, circle a word that has a **prefix** or a **suffix**. Then, write the prefix or suffix and the **root word**.

1. We stayed up late.

    _____ _____

    - - - - - - - - - - - - - - - - - - - + - - - - - - -

    _____ _____

2. That rule seems unfair.

    _____ _____

    - - - - - - - - + - - - - - - - - - - - - - - - - - - -

    _____ _____

3. Is that snake harmful to people?

    _____ _____

    - - - - - - - - - - - - - - - - - - - + - - - - - - -

    _____ _____

4. We saw a preview for the new movie.

    _____ _____

    - - - - - - - - + - - - - - - - - - - - - - - - - - - -

    _____ _____

Eight friends want to share four apples. Draw lines to divide the apples into equal shares for eight friends.

Add the **prefix** or **suffix** to the **root word** to make a new word.

(un) lucky _____   talk (ing) _____

kitten (s) _____   (mis) place _____

(re) visit _____   hope (ful) _____

Solve the word problems.

1. Ana played a game for 63 minutes in the morning. She played the same game for 8 minutes in the afternoon. How many minutes did she play in all?

_____ minutes

2. 100 crackers were in the box. 70 were eaten. How many crackers were left?

_____ crackers

Read the passage. Answer the questions.

Like people, dogs get dirty. Some dogs get a bath once a month. Baby soap is a good soap for cleaning dogs. Fill a tub with warm water. Get someone to hold the dog still in the tub. Then, wash the dog quickly.

1. How often do some dogs get a bath?

_____

_ _

_____

_____

_ _ _ _ _ _ _ _ _ _ _ _ _ _ _ _ _

2. What is a good soap to use on dogs? _____

_____

_ _ _ _ _ _ _ _ _ _ _ _ _ _ _ _ _

3. Do you think most dogs like to take baths? _____

Twelve friends want to share three pizzas. Draw lines to divide the pizzas into equal shares for 12 friends.

Try these fun ideas for summer learning.

Basic Skills

• On index cards, write words such as **beach**, **playground**, and **tag** that relate to summer activities. As your collection of cards grows, ask your child to categorize the words in different ways.

• Hide a small treat. Write step-by-step directions for finding it and challenge your child to follow them. Let your child write directions for you, too.

• When reading a book or watching a movie, pause and ask your child to think of three things that might happen next. Was one of your child's predictions correct? Talk about why or why not.

• During car trips, play "I Spy," but require players to say "similar to" or "opposite of" as a part of each clue.

• Collect leaves, stones, shells, and other natural treasures. Make a pattern with the items. Can your child continue the pattern?

Reading

• Visit the library regularly and allow your child to choose several books. As you read together, notice consonant blends, words, uppercase letters, and punctuation marks. Talk about the story.

• Ask your child to choose something interesting from one book, such as an animal, place, or activity. At the library, challenge him or her to find another book about that topic. Continue the chain.

• After watching a movie with your child, ask each other questions about it. Who can remember more details about the plot and characters? The player who stumps the other is the winner.

• Help your child set up a special place to read outside in nice weather. It could include a folding chair, a pillow, or a cold drink.

• After reading a book, invite your child to make a puppet play, drawing, or video about the story.

Writing

• Write uppercase and lowercase letters in the sand, with sidewalk chalk, and on a fence with paintbrushes dipped in water.

• Encourage your child to correspond via e-mail with a relative or friend who lives far away.

• Help your child make up a silly character and draw a picture of him or her. Suggest that your child write and illustrate stories about the character's silly summer adventures.

• On index cards, write nouns, verbs, adjectives, and other words that are meaningful to your child. Use the cards to build sentences.

• In a shoebox, place pencils, markers, envelopes, stickers, and other writing materials. Encourage your child to use the supplies often.

Math

• Write numbers to 120 on index cards. Use the cards to play "War" with your child.

• Fill each of 10 zip-top bags with 10 pieces of cereal or other small items. Use the bags along with single items to represent tens and ones in numbers from 1 to 120.

• During car trips, ask your child to identify the numbers on license plates and choose two of them to add or subtract.

• Have an "equal parts" picnic. Help your child cut food items into equal halves and fourths.

• Provide a yardstick. Help your child keep a running list of things that are shorter or longer than a yardstick.

Answer Key

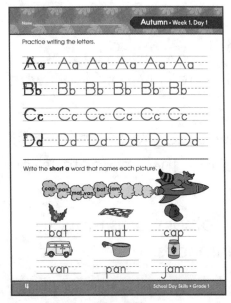

Page 4

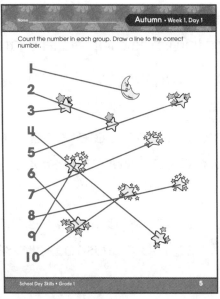

Page 5

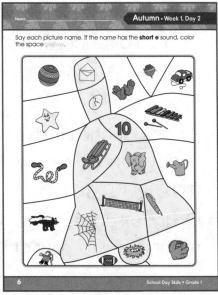

Page 6

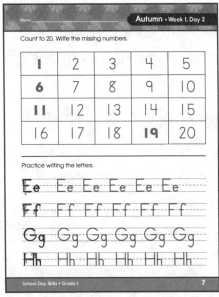

Page 7

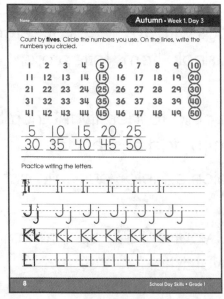

Page 8

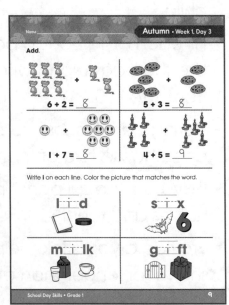

Page 9

School Day Skills • Grade 1

Answer Key

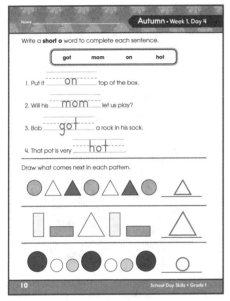

Page 10

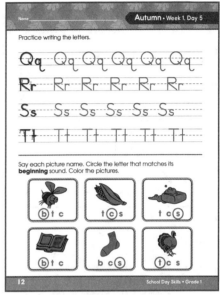

Page 11

Page 12

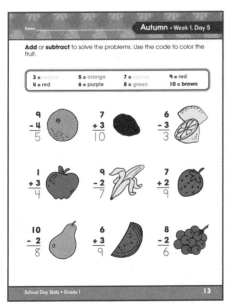

Page 13

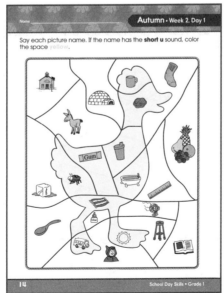

Page 14

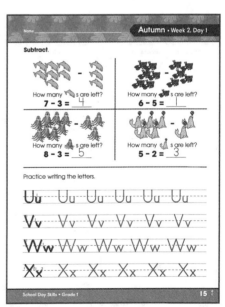

Page 15

Answer Key

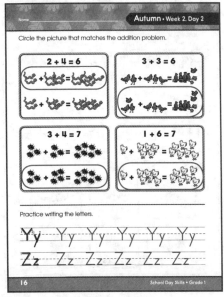

Page 16

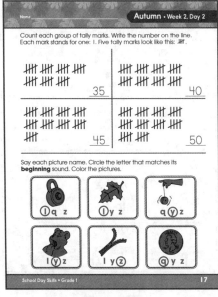

Page 17

Page 18

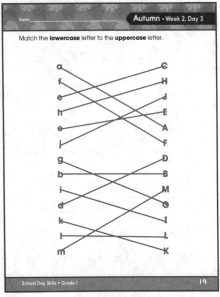

Page 19

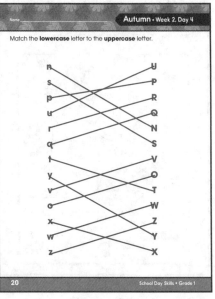

Page 20

Page 21

Answer Key

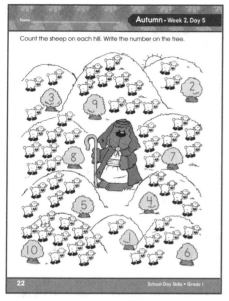

Page 22

Page 23

Page 24

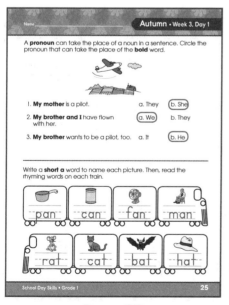

Page 25

Page 26

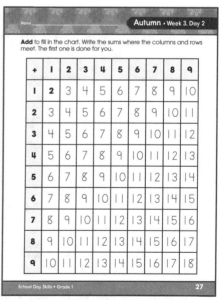

Page 27

Answer Key

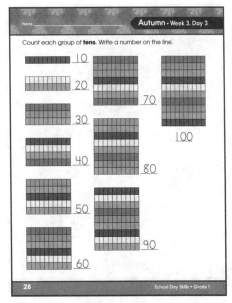

Page 28

Page 29

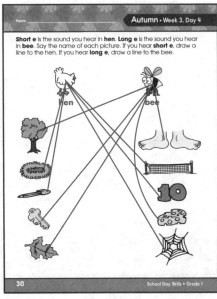

Page 30

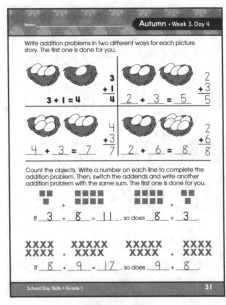

Page 31

Page 32

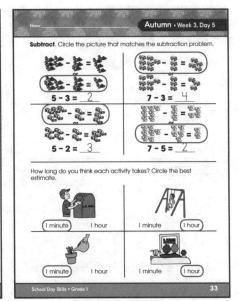

Page 33

Answer Key

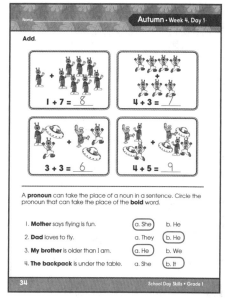

Page 34

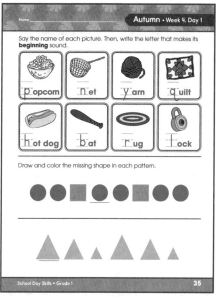

Page 35

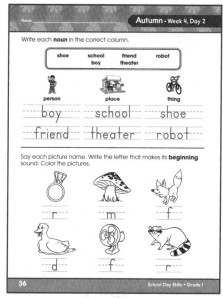

Page 36

Page 37

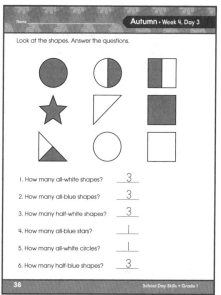

Page 38

Page 39

Answer Key

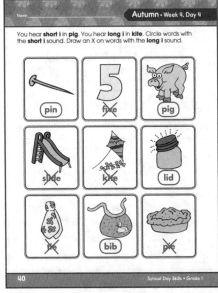

Page 40

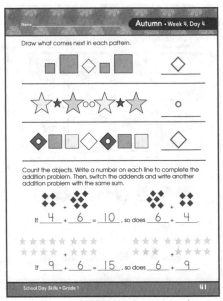

Page 41

Page 42

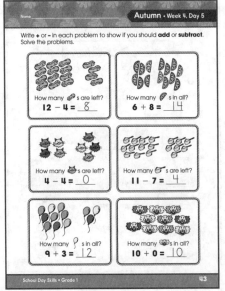

Page 43

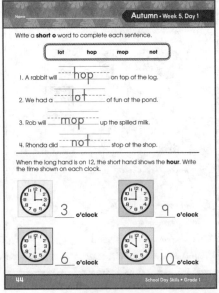

Page 44

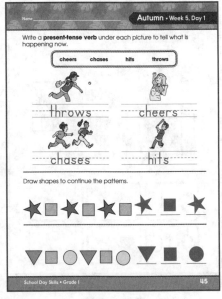

Page 45

Answer Key

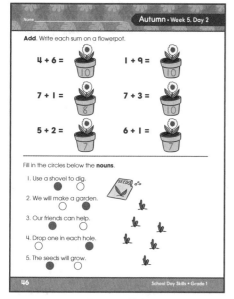

Page 46

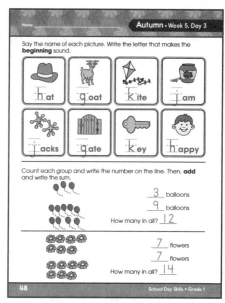

Page 47

Autumn • Week 5, Day 3

Page 48

Page 49

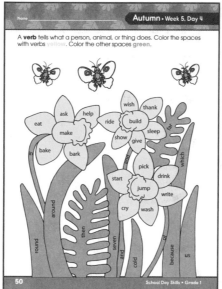

Page 50

Page 51

Answer Key

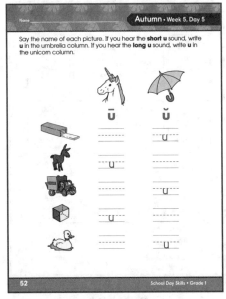

Page 52

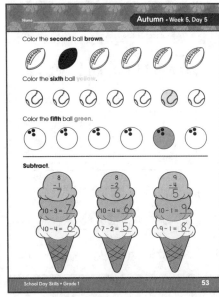

Page 53

Autumn • Week 6, Day 1

A **adjective** describes a person, place, or thing. Write an adjective to describe each picture.

| wet | round | sad | tall |

tall   round

sad   wet

Write **1** to **12** in the boxes to put the months in order. The first one is done for you.

4	April	2	February	5	May
10	October	7	July	8	August
12	December	1	January	3	March
9	September	6	June	11	November

Page 54

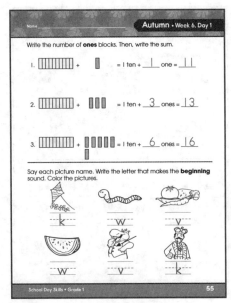

Page 55

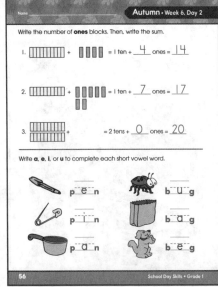

Page 56

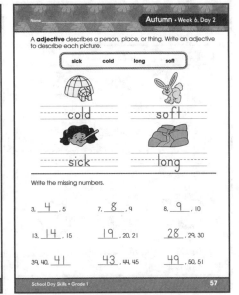

Page 57

Answer Key

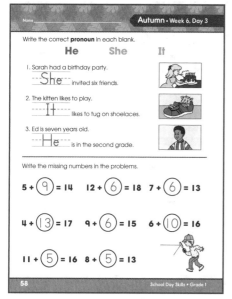

Page 58

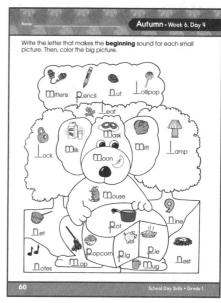

Page 59

Page 60

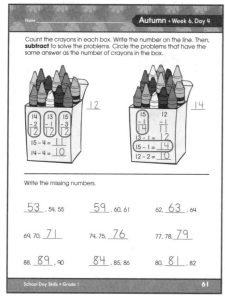

Page 61

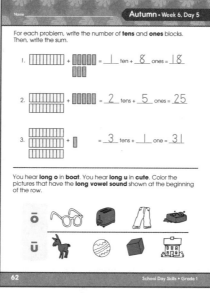

Page 62

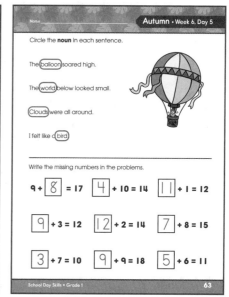

Page 63

Answer Key

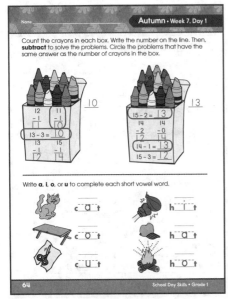

Page 64

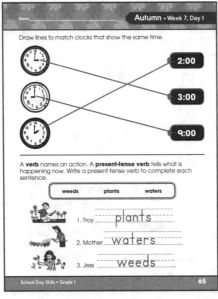

Page 65

Page 66

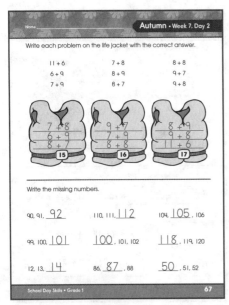

Page 67

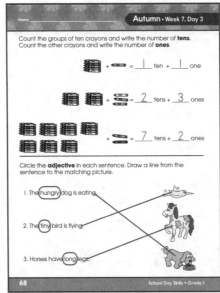

Page 68

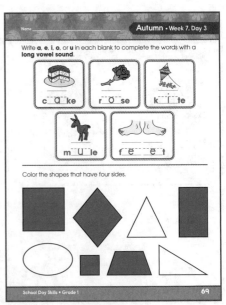

Page 69

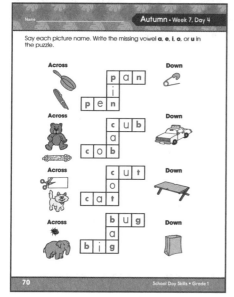

Page 70

Page 71

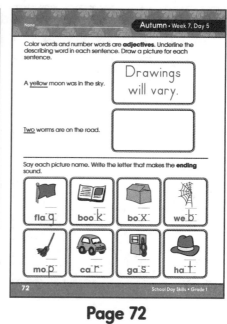

Page 72

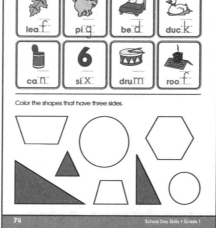

Page 73

Page 74

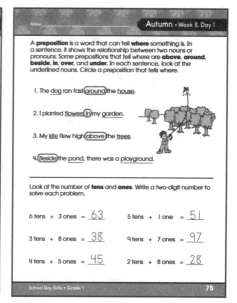

Page 75

Answer Key

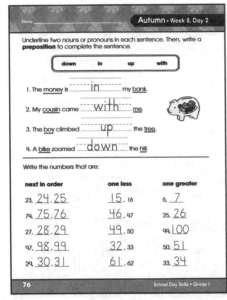

Page 76

Autumn • Week 8, Day 2

Underline two nouns or pronouns in each sentence. Then, write a **preposition** to complete the sentence.

down	in	up	with

1. The money is __in__ my bank.
2. My cousin came __with__ me.
3. The boy climbed __up__ the tree.
4. A bike zoomed __down__ the hill.

Write the numbers that are:

next in order	one less	one greater
23. 24. 25	15. 16	6. 7
74. 75. 76	46. 47	25. 26
27. 28. 29	49. 50	99. 100
97. 98. 99	32. 33	50. 51
29. 30. 31	61. 62	33. 34

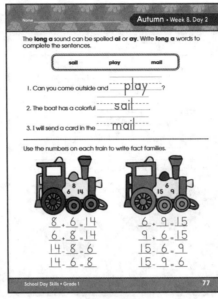

Page 77

Autumn • Week 8, Day 2

The **long a** sound can be spelled **ai** or **ay**. Write long a words to complete the sentences.

sail	play	mail

1. Can you come outside and __play__?
2. The boat has a colorful __sail__.
3. I will send a card in the __mail__.

Use the numbers on each train to write fact families.

8 + 6 = 14
6 + 8 = 14
14 - 8 = 6
14 - 6 = 8

6 + 9 = 15
9 + 6 = 15
15 - 6 = 9
15 - 9 = 6

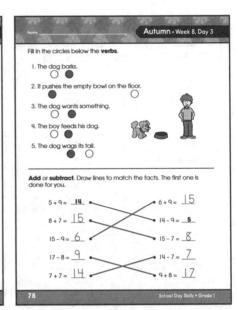

Page 78

Autumn • Week 8, Day 3

Fill in the circles below the **verbs**.

1. The dog barks.
2. It pushes the empty bowl on the floor.
3. The dog wants something.
4. The boy feeds his dog.
5. The dog wags its tail.

Add or **subtract**. Draw lines to match the facts. The first one is done for you.

5 + 9 = 14
8 + 7 = 15
15 - 9 = 6
17 - 8 = 9
7 + 7 = 14

6 + 9 = 15
14 - 9 = 5
15 - 7 = 8
14 - 7 = 7
9 + 8 = 17

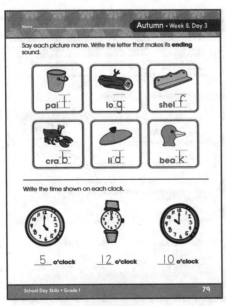

Page 79

Autumn • Week 8, Day 3

Say each picture name. Write the letter that makes its **ending** sound.

pai **t**   lo **g**   shel **f**
cra **b**   li **d**   bea **k**

Write the time shown on each clock.

__5__ o'clock   __12__ o'clock   __10__ o'clock

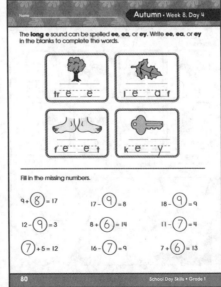

Page 80

Autumn • Week 8, Day 4

The **long e** sound can be spelled **ee**, **ea**, or **ey**. Write **ee**, **ea**, or **ey** in the blanks to complete the words.

tr **ee**   l **ea** f
f **ee** t   k **ey**

Fill in the missing numbers.

9 + ⑧ = 17   17 - ⑨ = 8   18 - ⑨ = 9
12 - ⑨ = 3   8 + ⑥ = 14   11 - ⑦ = 4
⑦ + 5 = 12   16 - ⑦ = 9   7 + ⑥ = 13

Page 81

Autumn • Week 8, Day 4

Connect the dots to draw three shapes that have four sides.

Answers will vary.

A sentence that tells something ends with a **period** (.). Write the **telling sentences**. Begin each one with an uppercase letter. End each one with a period.

this dog is friendly

This dog is friendly.

the bird came to me

The bird came to me.

Answer Key

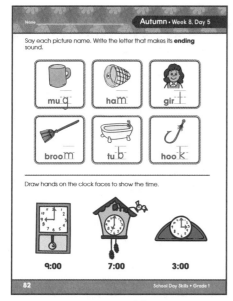

Page 82

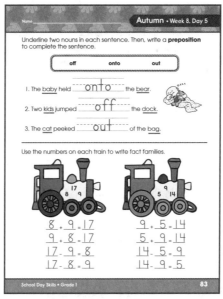

Page 83

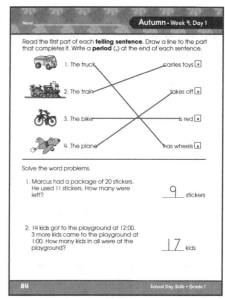

Page 84

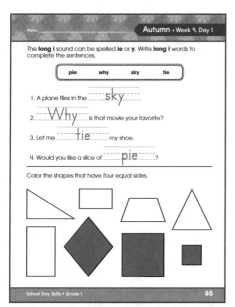

Page 85

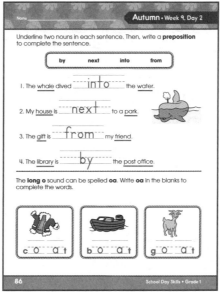

Page 86

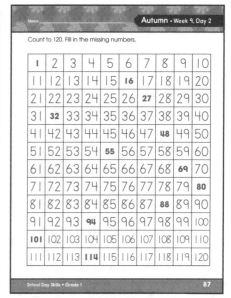

Page 87

Answer Key

Autumn • Week 9, Day 3

Say the name of each picture. Write a letter that spells its **beginning** sound, **middle** sound, and **ending** sound. Color the pictures.

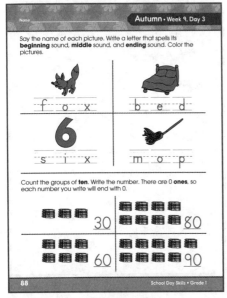

f o x | b e d

6

s i x | m o p

Count the groups of **ten**. Write the number. There are 0 **ones**, so each number you write will end with 0.

30 | 80

60 | 90

88   School Day Skills • Grade 1

Page 88

Autumn • Week 9, Day 3

A sentence that asks something ends with a **question mark (?)**. Write the **asking sentences**. Begin each one with an uppercase letter. End each one with a question mark.

do you like to read

Do you like to read?

what is that book about

What is that book about?

Solve the word problems.

1. Kelsey solved 9 clues for a puzzle. There are 18 clues in all. How many more clues does Kelsey have to solve? ___9___ clues

2. Dad made 10 tacos. He made 6 burritos. How many items did he make in all? ___16___ items

School Day Skills • Grade 1   89

Page 89

Autumn • Week 9, Day 4

The **long u** sound can be spelled **ue** or **ew**. Write **long u** words to complete the sentences.

| few | blue | new | true |

1. A fact is __true__
2. His eyes are __blue__
3. I need __new__ shoes.
4. Stay a __few__ minutes.

An **article** is a small word that comes before a noun. **A** and **an** are articles. Write **a** before a word that begins with a consonant letter. Write **an** before a word that begins with a vowel letter. Write **a** or **an** to complete each sentence.

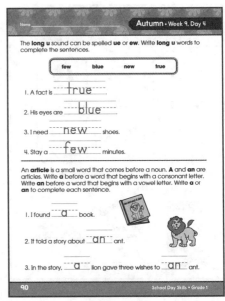

1. I found __a__ book.

2. It told a story about __an__ ant.

3. In the story, __a__ lion gave three wishes to __an__ ant.

90   School Day Skills • Grade 1

Page 90

Autumn • Week 9, Day 4

Use the code to color the shapes.

School Day Skills • Grade 1   91

Page 91

Autumn • Week 9, Day 5

Write the first word of each **asking sentence**. It should begin with an uppercase letter. Write a **question mark** to end each sentence.

| can | do | what |

1. __Can__ we feed the ducks [?]

2. __Do__ you see the monkeys [?]

3. __What__ time will we eat lunch [?]

Solve the word problems.

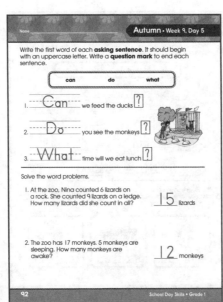

1. At the zoo, Nina counted 6 lizards on a rock. She counted 9 lizards on a ledge. How many lizards did she count in all? __15__ lizards

2. The zoo has 17 monkeys. 5 monkeys are sleeping. How many monkeys are awake? __12__ monkeys

92   School Day Skills • Grade 1

Page 92

Autumn • Week 9, Day 5

Say the name of each picture. Write a letter that matches its **beginning** sound, **middle** sound, and **ending** sound. Color the pictures.

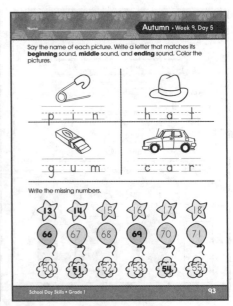

p i n | h a t

g u m | c a r

Write the missing numbers.

13 14 15 16 17 18
66 67 68 69 70 71
50 51 52 53 54 55

School Day Skills • Grade 1   93

Page 93

Answer Key

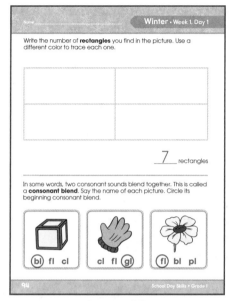

Page 94

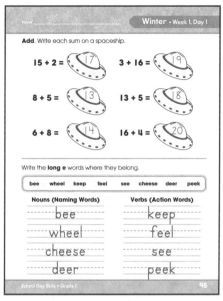

Page 95

Page 96

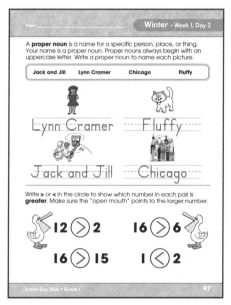

Page 97

Page 94

Name _____ Winter • Week 1, Day 1

Write the number of **rectangles** you find in the picture. Use a different color to trace each one.

_7_ rectangles

In some words, two consonant sounds blend together. This is called a **consonant blend**. Say the name of each picture. Circle its beginning consonant blend.

(bl) fl cl   cl fl (gl)   (fl) bl pl

94   School Day Skills • Grade 1

Page 95

Name _____ Winter • Week 1, Day 1

Add. Write each sum on a spaceship.

15 + 2 = 17   3 + 16 = 19
8 + 5 = 13   13 + 5 = 18
6 + 8 = 14   16 + 4 = 20

Write the **long e** words where they belong.

| bee | wheel | keep | feel | see | cheese | deer | peek |

Nouns (Naming Words) | **Verbs (Action Words)**
bee | keep
wheel | feel
cheese | see
deer | peek

School Day Skills • Grade 1   95

Page 96

Name _____ Winter • Week 1, Day 2

Subtract. Write each difference on a beehive.

20 - 3 = 17   20 - 5 = 15
11 - 6 = 5   13 - 8 = 5
18 - 2 = 16   16 - 16 = 0

Say the name of each picture. Circle its beginning **consonant blend**.

fl (cl) gl   (pl) gl cl   gl fl (sl)

96   School Day Skills • Grade 1

Page 97

Name _____ Winter • Week 1, Day 2

A **proper noun** is a name for a specific person, place, or thing. Your name is a proper noun. Proper nouns always begin with an uppercase letter. Write a proper noun to name each picture.

| Jack and Jill | Lynn Cramer | Chicago | Fluffy |

Lynn Cramer   Fluffy
Jack and Jill   Chicago

Write **>** or **<** in the circle to show which number in each pair is **greater**. Make sure the "open mouth" points to the larger number.

12 (>) 2   16 (>) 6
16 (>) 15   1 (<) 2

School Day Skills • Grade 1   97

Page 98

Name _____ Winter • Week 1, Day 3

Write a **consonant blend** to begin each word.

tr ain   fr og   cr ab

Write the number that matches each group of **tens** and **ones**.

4 tens 6 ones 46   3 tens 2 ones 32
2 tens 9 ones 29   4 tens 0 ones 40
1 ten 4 ones 14   0 tens 6 ones 6
2 tens 1 one 21   4 tens 7 ones 47
3 tens 3 ones 33   1 ten 1 one 11

98   School Day Skills • Grade 1

Page 99

Name _____ Winter • Week 1, Day 3

A **past-tense verb** tells about an action that already happened. Add **ed** to most verbs to show the past tense. Write the past tense of each verb. The first one is done for you.

1. push   pushed
2. want   wanted
3. help   helped
4. heat   heated
5. color   colored
6. pull   pulled

Write any numbers to make the addition problems true.

___ + ___ = 7   ___ + ___ = 9
___ + ___ = 7   Answers   ___ + ___ = 9
___ + ___ = 11   will vary.   ___ + ___ = 12
___ + ___ = 11   ___ + ___ = 12

School Day Skills • Grade 1   99

Answer Key

Page 100

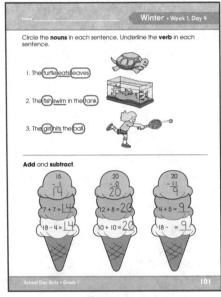

Page 101

Page 102

Page 103

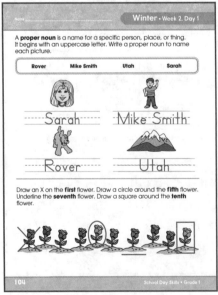

Page 104

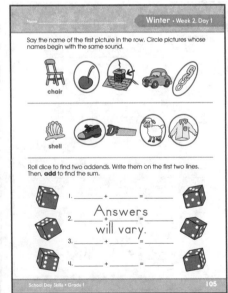

Page 105

Answer Key

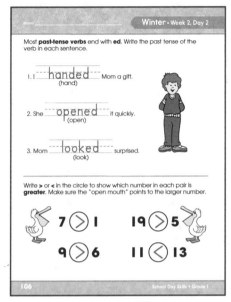

Page 106

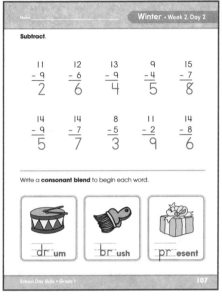

Page 107

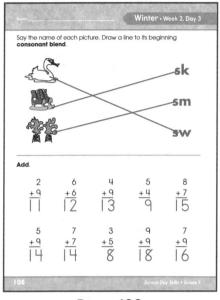

Page 108

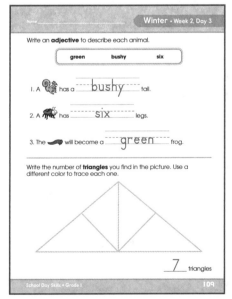

Page 109

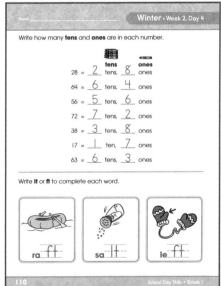

Page 110

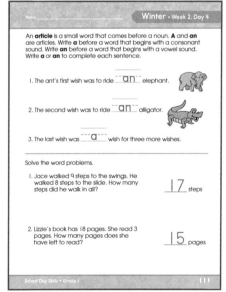

Page 111

Answer Key

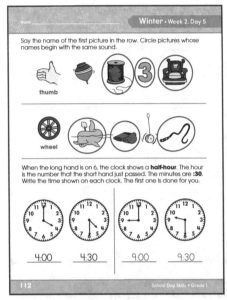

Page 112

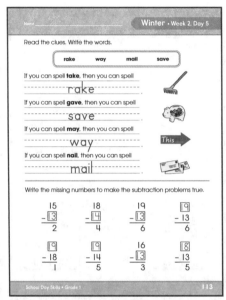

Page 113

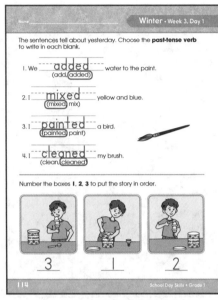

Page 114

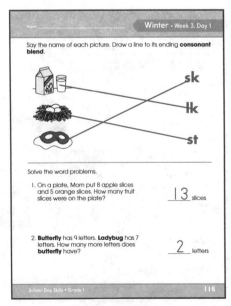

Page 115

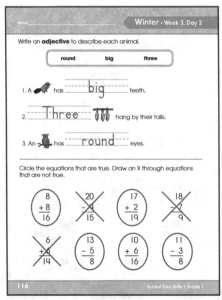

Page 116

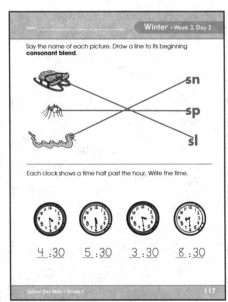

Page 117

294

School Day Skills • Grade 1

Answer Key

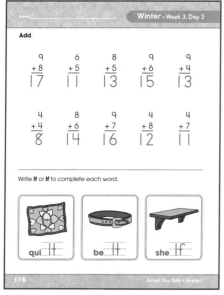

Page 118

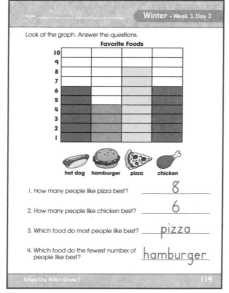

Page 119

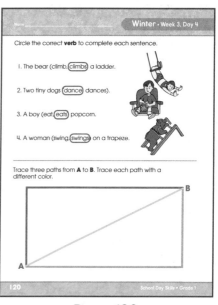

Page 120

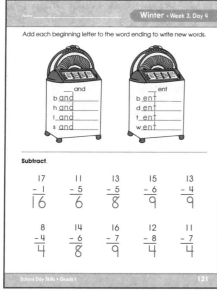

Page 121

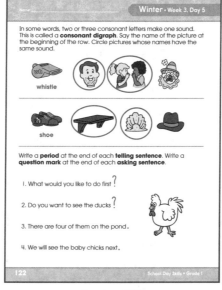

Page 122

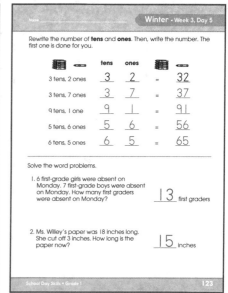

Page 123

Answer Key

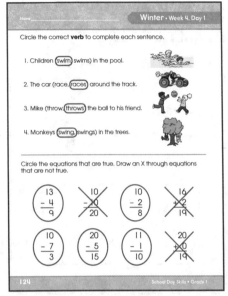

Page 124

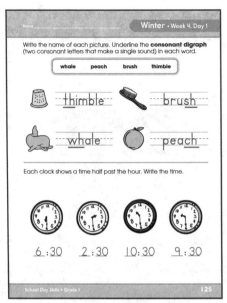

Page 125

Winter • Week 4, Day 2

Rewrite the dates. Begin the name of each month with an uppercase letter. Use a **comma** to separate the day and the year. The first one is done for you.

1. On april 17 2005, we saw the Grand Canyon.
   April 17, 2005

2. Our vacation started on april 2 2002.
   April 2, 2002

3. Molly's sister was born on august 14 2011.
   August 14, 2011

Add.

4	5	4	9	7
+6	+3	+5	+9	+3
10	8	9	18	10
6	7	3	6	2
+6	+8	+8	+3	+6
12	15	11	9	8

Page 126

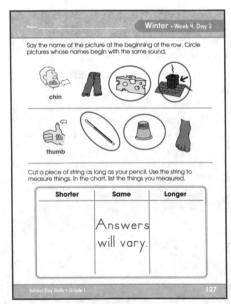

Page 127

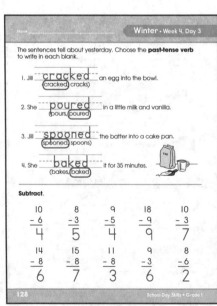

Page 128

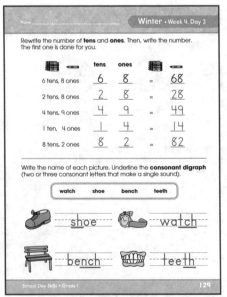

Page 129

School Day Skills • Grade 1

Answer Key

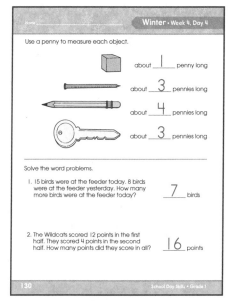

Page 130

Page 131

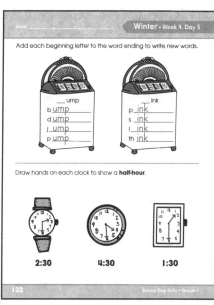

Page 132

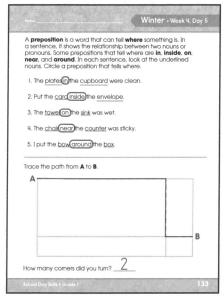

Page 133

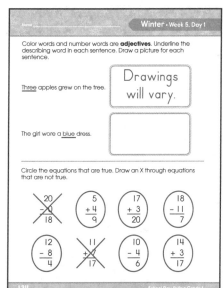

Page 134

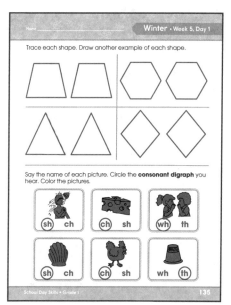

Page 135

Answer Key

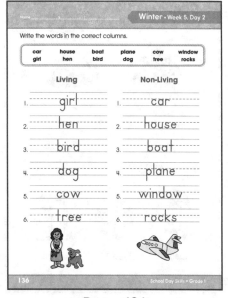

Page 136

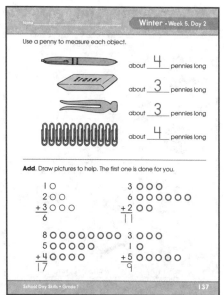

Page 137

Page 138

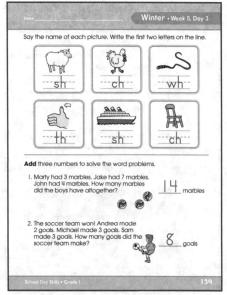

Page 139

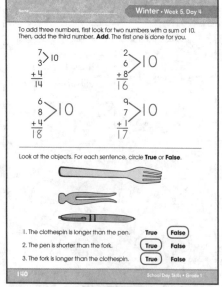

Page 140

Page 141

Answer Key

Color the ☆s yellow. Color the ○s **red**. Color the ☾s **blue**. Color the ◇s **purple**. Write the number you count for each shape.

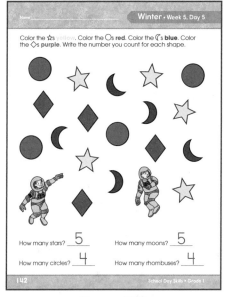

How many stars? 5

How many circles? 4

How many moons? 5

How many rhombuses? 4

Page 142

A **possessive pronoun** shows ownership. Rewrite the sentences with the possessive pronoun in place of the **bold** words.

1. That is **Lisa's** book. (her)

That is her book.

2. This is **my pencil**. (mine)

This is mine.

Say the name of each picture. Then, write a **rhyming** word.

| chop | chain | chin | chase |

chase

chain

chop

chin

Page 143

How many different shapes can you find in the picture? Trace each shape with a different color.

2 triangles
4 rectangles
1 square

Add. Draw pictures to help. The first one is done for you.

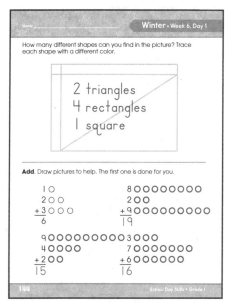

Page 144

Write the category that describes each group of words.

| clothes | flowers | colors |

rose	green	shirt
buttercup	purple	socks
tulip	blue	dress
daisy	red	coat

flowers

colors

clothes

Color each space that has an **adjective**, or describing word.

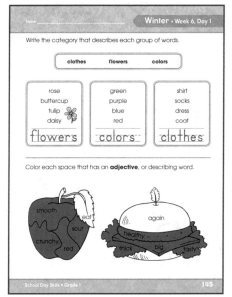

Page 145

Add three numbers to solve the word problems.

1. The first grade ran in three races. Team A scored 5 points. Team B scored 6 points. Team C scored 8 points. How many points did the first grade score?

19 points

2. We went to the farm. We saw 6 black pigs. We saw 4 black and white cows. We saw 6 brown hens. How many animals did we see at the farm?

16 animals

Say the name of each picture. Write the first two letters on the line.

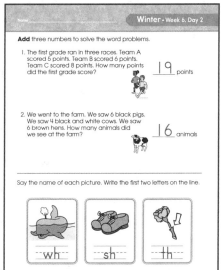

wh

sh

th

Page 146

Draw lines to match clocks that show the same time.

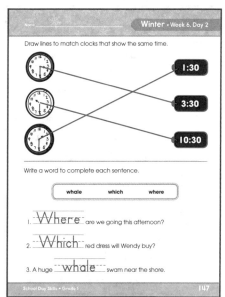

1:30

3:30

10:30

Write a word to complete each sentence.

| whale | which | where |

1. Where are we going this afternoon?

2. Which red dress will Wendy buy?

3. A huge whale swam near the shore.

Page 147

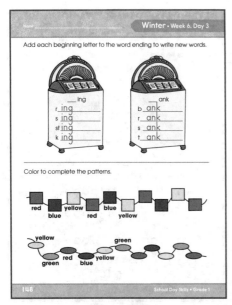

Page 148

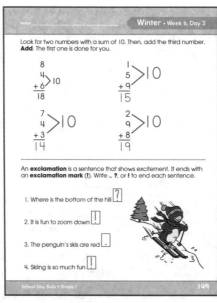

Page 149

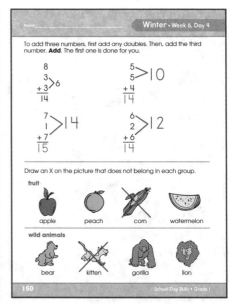

Page 150

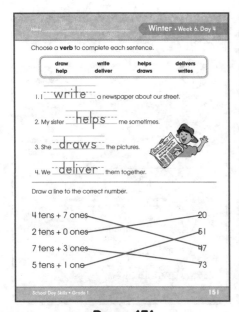

Page 151

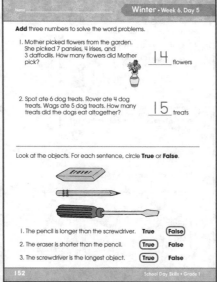

Page 152

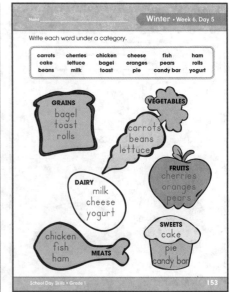

Page 153

Answer Key

Say each **long vowel** word. Write a vowel letter to complete it.

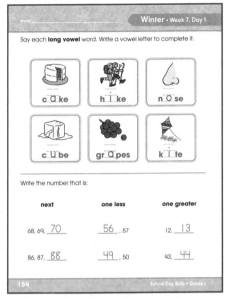

c a ke   h i ke   n o se

c u be   gr a pes   k i te

Write the number that is:

next	one less	one greater
68, 69, _70_	_56_, 57	12, _13_
86, 87, _88_	_49_, 50	43, _44_

154   School Day Skills • Grade 1

Page 154

First, add any doubles. Then, add the third number. **Add.** The first one is done for you.

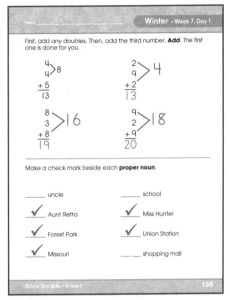

$\begin{matrix}4\\4\end{matrix}\rangle 8$ $\begin{matrix}2\\2\end{matrix}\rangle 4$
+5 / 13   +9 / 13

$\begin{matrix}8\\3\end{matrix}\rangle 16$ $\begin{matrix}9\\2\end{matrix}\rangle 18$
+8 / 19   +9 / 20

Make a check mark beside each **proper noun**.

____ uncle   ____ school

✓ Aunt Retta   ✓ Miss Hunter

✓ Forest Park   ✓ Union Station

✓ Missouri   ____ shopping mall

School Day Skills • Grade 1   155

Page 155

Unscramble the words. In each word, the **long vowel sound** is spelled with two vowel letters together.

ocat coat   eetf feet

mtea meat   apil pail

Complete the number patterns.

1. 5, _10_, _15_, 20, _25_, _30_, 35, _40_, _45_, 50

2. _2_, 4, 6, _8_, _10_, 12, _14_, 16, _18_, _20_

3. 10, _20_, _30_, 40, _50_, _60_, 70, _80_, 90

4. 4, _8_, 12, _16_, _20_, 24, _28_, 32, _36_, 40

156   School Day Skills • Grade 1

Page 156

Add. Break up each problem into two smaller problems. The first one is done for you.

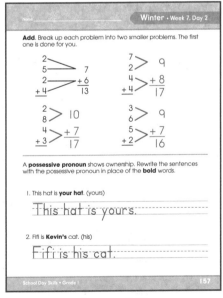

$\begin{matrix}2\\5\end{matrix}\rangle 7$ $\begin{matrix}7\\2\end{matrix}\rangle 9$
$\begin{matrix}2\\+4\end{matrix}\rangle$ +6 / 13 $\begin{matrix}4\\+4\end{matrix}\rangle$ +8 / 17

$\begin{matrix}2\\8\end{matrix}\rangle 10$ $\begin{matrix}3\\6\end{matrix}\rangle 9$
$\begin{matrix}4\\+3\end{matrix}\rangle$ +7 / 17 $\begin{matrix}5\\+2\end{matrix}\rangle$ +7 / 16

A **possessive pronoun** shows ownership. Rewrite the sentences with the possessive pronoun in place of the **bold** words.

1. This hat is **your** hat. (yours)

This hat is yours.

2. Fifi is **Kevin's** cat. (his)

Fifi is his cat.

School Day Skills • Grade 1   157

Page 157

Write the category that describes each group of words.

| animals | toys | fruits |

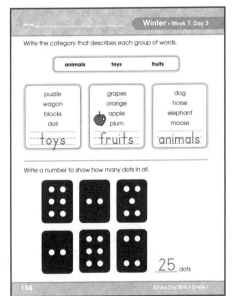

| puzzle wagon blocks doll | grapes orange apple plum | dog horse elephant moose |
| toys | fruits | animals |

Write a number to show how many dots in all.

25 dots

158   School Day Skills • Grade 1

Page 158

Count the tally marks. Write the number.

13   20

17   8

Use tally marks to represent the numbers.

15 |||| |||| |||| 22 |||| |||| |||| |||| ||

A **command** is a sentence that tells what to do. It begins with a **verb**. A command can end with a period (.) or an exclamation mark (!). Underline each sentence that gives a command.

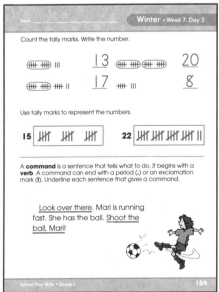

<u>Look over there</u>. Mari is running fast. She has the ball. <u>Shoot the ball, Mari!</u>

School Day Skills • Grade 1   159

Page 159

Answer Key

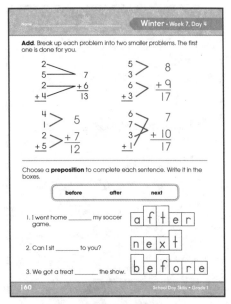

Page 160

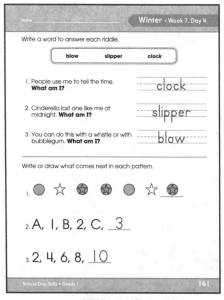

Page 161

Page 162

Page 163

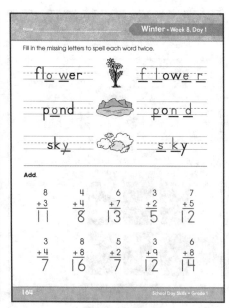

Page 164

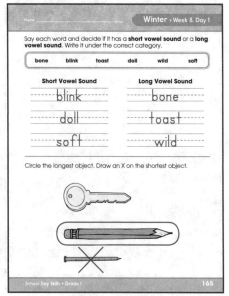

Page 165

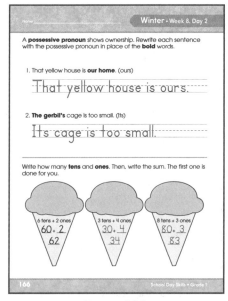

Page 166

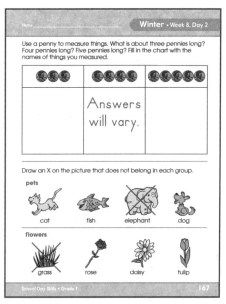

Page 167

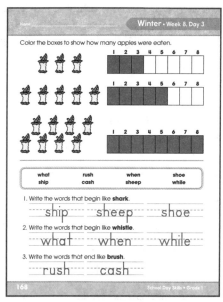

Page 168

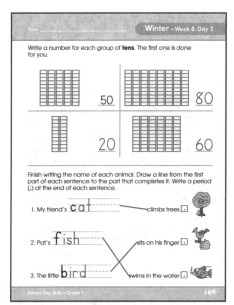

Page 169

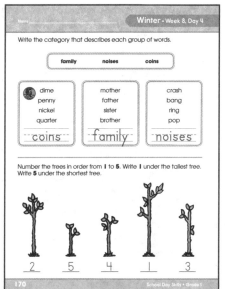

Page 170

Page 171

Answer Key

Page 172

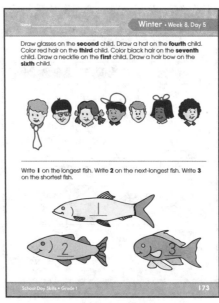

Page 173

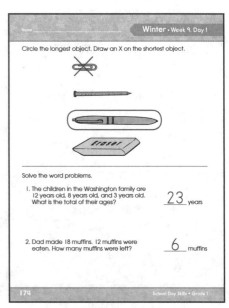

Page 174

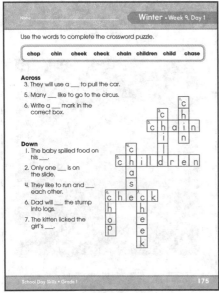

Page 175

Page 176

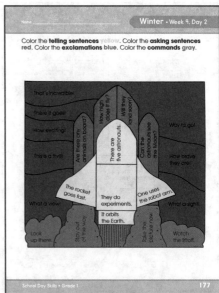

Page 177

Answer Key

Page 178

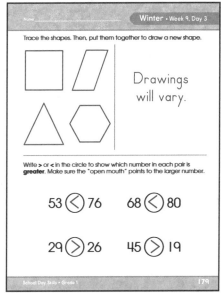

Page 179

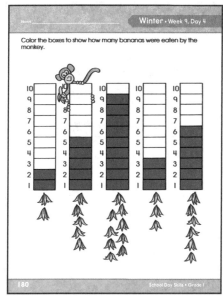

Page 180

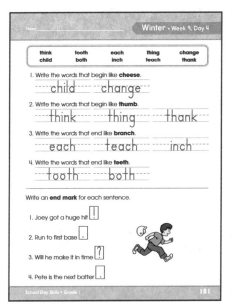

Page 181

Page 182

Page 183 content

Write T beside the **telling sentence**. Write A beside the **asking sentence**. Write E beside the **exclamation**. Write C beside the **command**.

T Two different kinds of penguins live in Antarctica.

A Do emperor penguins have black and white bodies?

C Look at their webbed feet.

E They are amazing!

Write the number that makes each equation true.

$$\begin{array}{r}20\\-\boxed{16}\\\hline 4\end{array}\qquad\begin{array}{r}\boxed{7}\\+\ 8\\\hline 15\end{array}\qquad\begin{array}{r}7\\-\boxed{0}\\\hline 7\end{array}\qquad\begin{array}{r}5\\+11\\\hline \boxed{16}\end{array}$$

$$\begin{array}{r}15\\-\boxed{6}\\\hline 9\end{array}\qquad\begin{array}{r}\boxed{10}\\+10\\\hline 20\end{array}\qquad\begin{array}{r}\boxed{15}\\-11\\\hline 4\end{array}\qquad\begin{array}{r}17\\+\ 2\\\hline \boxed{19}\end{array}$$

Page 183

Answer Key

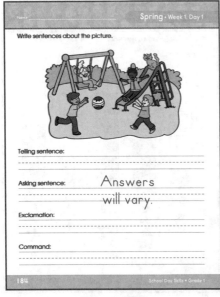

Page 184

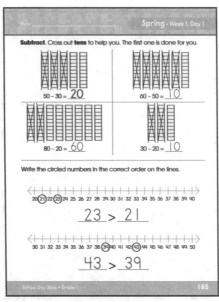

Page 185

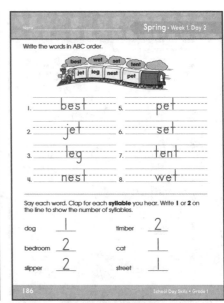

Page 186

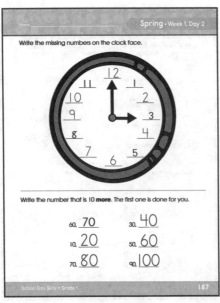

Page 187

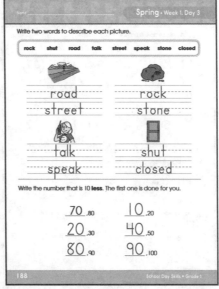

Page 188

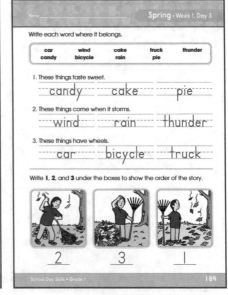

Page 189

Answer Key

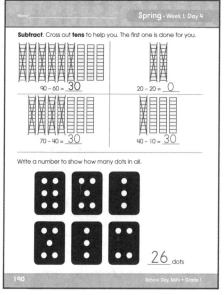

Page 190

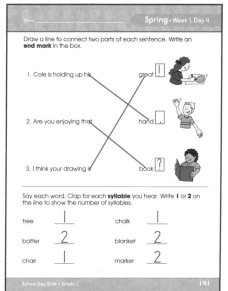

Page 191

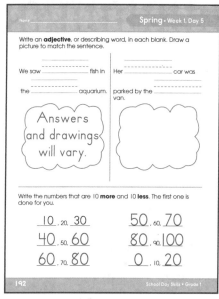

Page 192

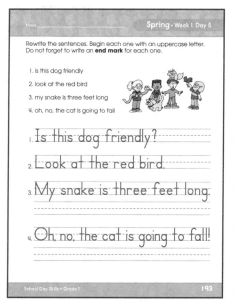

Page 193

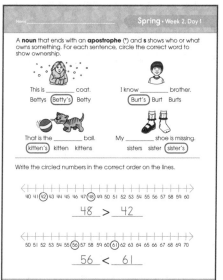

Page 194

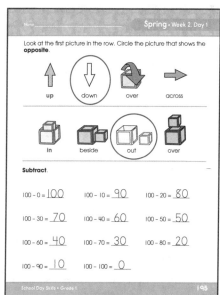

Page 195

Answer Key

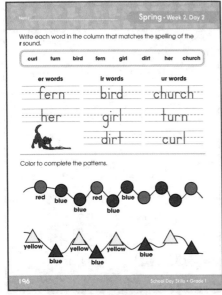

Page 196

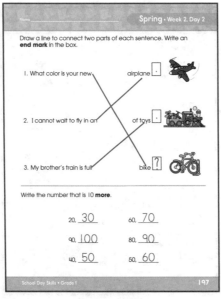

Page 197

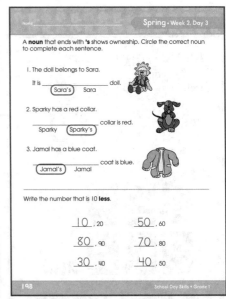

Page 198

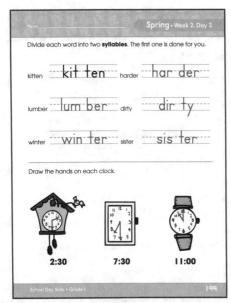

Page 199

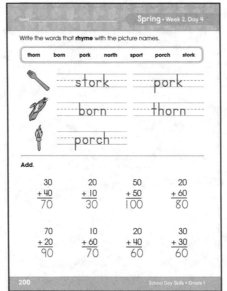

Page 200

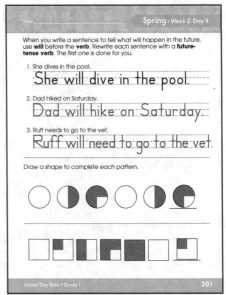

Page 201

Answer Key

Circle the correct word to complete each sentence.

1. The _____ lunch box is broken. (boy's) boys

2. _____ hair is brown. Anns (Ann's)

3. The _____ fur is black. (cat's) cats

4. The _____ paws are muddy. dogs (dog's)

Subtract.

100	40	70	80
− 40	− 10	− 60	− 50
60	30	10	30

90	100	70	30
− 40	− 20	− 20	− 30
50	80	50	0

Page 202

Write the words in ABC order.

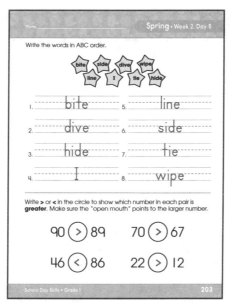

1. bite   5. line
2. dive   6. side
3. hide   7. tie
4. I   8. wipe

Write **>** or **<** in the circle to show which number in each pair is **greater**. Make sure the "open mouth" points to the larger number.

90 (>) 89   70 (>) 67

46 (<) 86   22 (>) 12

Page 203

Rewrite each sentence with a **future-tense verb**. The first one is done for you.

1. Marty wiped the counter.
   Marty will wipe the counter.

2. Suki helps wash the car.
   Suki will help wash the car.

3. The lady painted my face.
   The lady will paint my face.

Write the time shown on each clock.

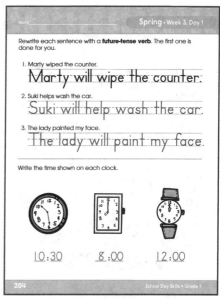

10:30   8:00   12:00

Page 204

Circle the word that is spelled correctly. Write it on the line.

(touch) fuch touh —— touch

smel (smell) smell —— smell

her (hear) har —— hear

Add the **tens** and **ones**. Write the sum. The first one is done for you.

2 tens and 6 ones	1 ten and 4 ones
+ 1 ten and 0 ones	+ 3 tens and 0 ones
3 tens and 6 ones = 36	4 tens and 4 ones = 44

7 tens and 3 ones	1 ten and 6 ones
+ 2 tens and 0 ones	+ 3 tens and 0 ones
9 tens and 3 ones = 93	4 tens and 6 ones = 46

Page 205

Circle the correct word to complete each sentence.

1. The _____ cage needs to be cleaned. gerbils (gerbil's)

2. My _____ coat is torn. (sister's) sister

3. The _____ neck is long. giraffes (giraffe's)

4. The _____ paws are big and powerful. (lion's) lions

Color the boxes to show how many spots are on each turtle's shell.

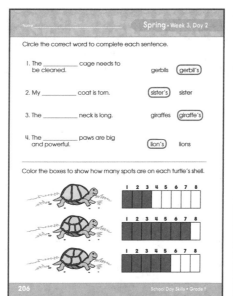

Page 206

Choose the word that describes the picture. Write it on the line.

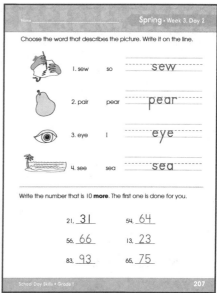

1. sew so —— sew

2. pair pear —— pear

3. eye I —— eye

4. see sea —— sea

Write the number that is 10 **more**. The first one is done for you.

21. 31   54. 64

56. 66   13. 23

83. 93   65. 75

Page 207

Answer Key

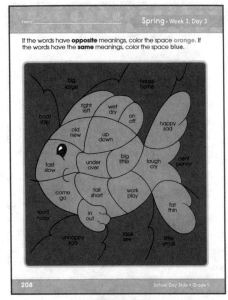

Page 208

Page 209

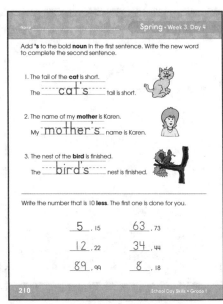

Page 210

Page 211

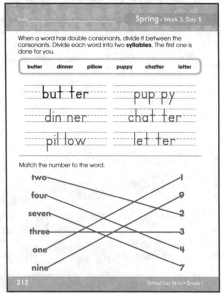

Page 212

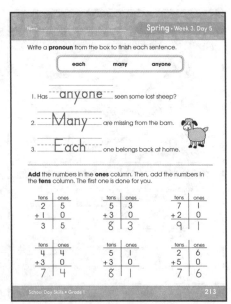

Page 213

Answer Key

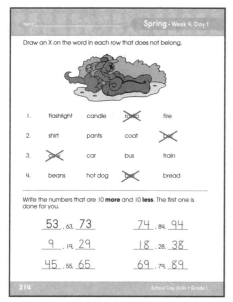

Page 214

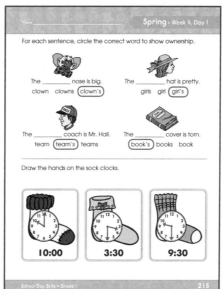

Page 215

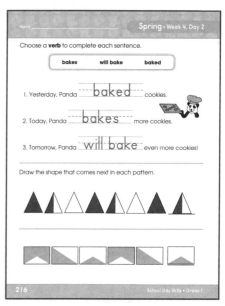

Page 216

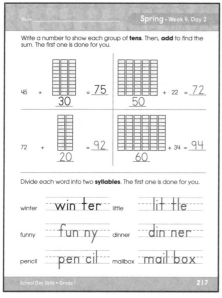

Page 217

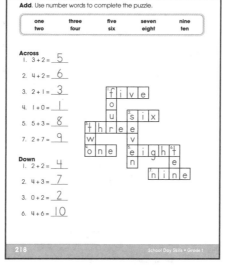

Page 218

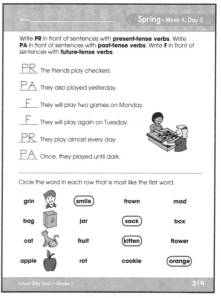

Page 219

Answer Key

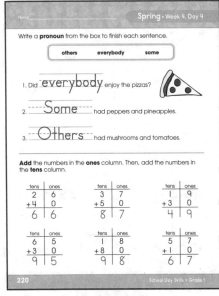

Page 220

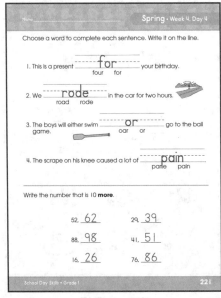

Page 221

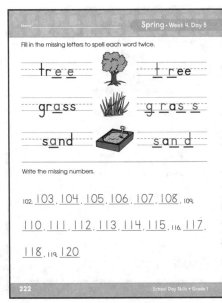

Page 222

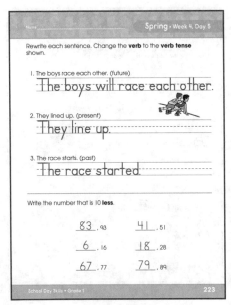

Page 223

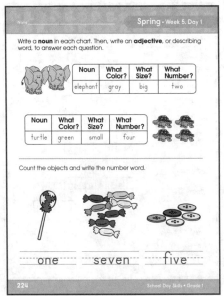

Page 224

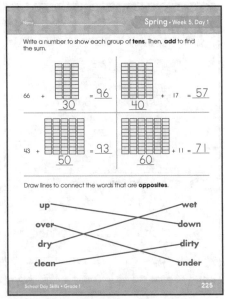

Page 225

Answer Key

Page 226

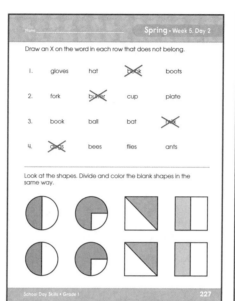

Page 227

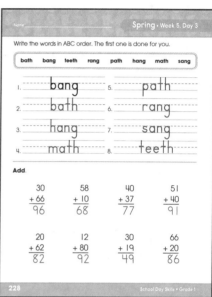

Page 228

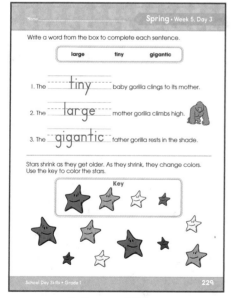

Page 229

Page 230

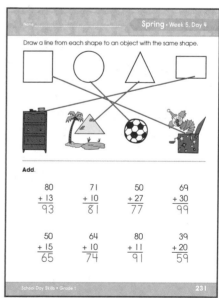

Page 231

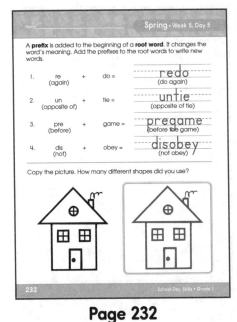

Page 232

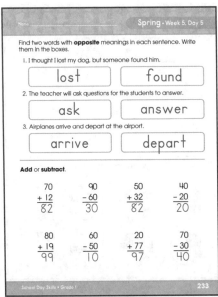

Page 233

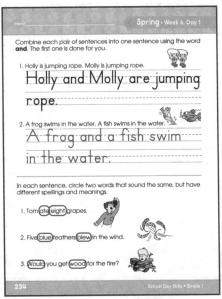

Page 234

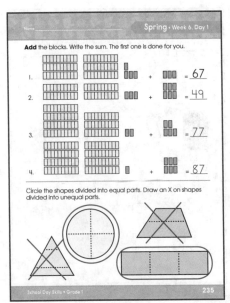

Page 235

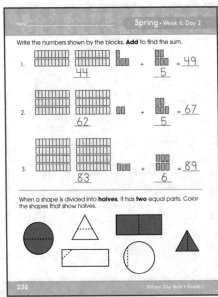

Page 236

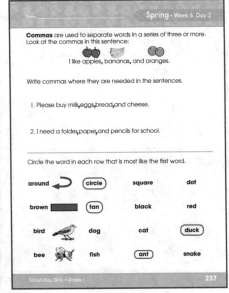

Page 237

Answer Key

Page 238

Name ___

Spring • Week 6, Day 3

Add a **prefix** to the **root word** in each sentence.

| un | mis | dis | im |

1. Do you **dis**agree with me?

2. I found a **mis**take.

3. This puzzle is **im**possible!

4. The **un**happy toddler screamed.

Add the **ones**. Then, add the **tens**.

tens	ones
3	3
+	5
3	8

tens	ones
7	4
+	4
7	8

tens	ones
8	4
+	2
8	6

tens	ones
7	5
+	4
7	9

tens	ones
1	2
+	6
1	8

tens	ones
5	5
+	1
5	6

238   School Day Skills • Grade 1

Page 238

Page 239

Name ___

Spring • Week 6, Day 3

Combine each pair of sentences into one sentence using the word **and**. The first one is done for you.

1. The truck has wheels. The bike has wheels.

The truck and bike have wheels.

2. Rosa has a ticket. I have a ticket.

Rosa and I have a ticket.

Look at the shapes. Divide and color the blank shapes in the same way.

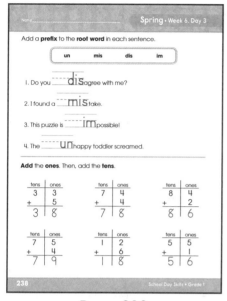

School Day Skills • Grade 1   239

Page 239

Page 240

Name ___

Spring • Week 6, Day 4

Complete the chart.

Prefix	Root Word	New Word
dis	like	dislike
un	done	undone
pre	pay	prepay
in	active	inactive
mis	take	mistake

Add the **ones**. Then, add the **tens**.

tens	ones
1	0
+	9
1	9

tens	ones
2	8
+	1
2	9

tens	ones
6	7
+	2
6	9

tens	ones
3	2
+	7
3	9

tens	ones
6	6
+	3
6	9

tens	ones
7	2
+	7
7	9

240   School Day Skills • Grade 1

Page 240

Page 241

Name ___

Spring • Week 6, Day 4

Write **commas** where they are needed in the sentences.

1. Some good pets are cats, dogs, gerbils, fish, and rabbits.

2. Aaron, Mike, and Matt went to the baseball game.

3. Major forms of transportation are planes, trains, and automobiles.

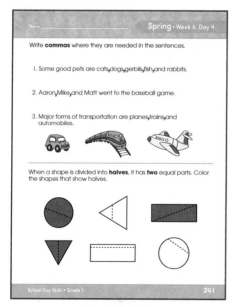

When a shape is divided into **halves**, it has **two** equal parts. Color the shapes that show halves.

School Day Skills • Grade 1   241

Page 241

Page 242

Name ___

Spring • Week 6, Day 5

Divide each word into two **syllables** between two consonant letters. The first one is done for you.

| window | mister | barber | doctor | winter | sister |

win dow   doc tor

mis ter   win ter

bar ber   sis ter

Color one **half** of each shape.

242   School Day Skills • Grade 1

Page 242

Page 243

Name ___

Spring • Week 6, Day 5

Combine each pair of sentences into one sentence using the word **and**. The first one is done for you.

1. Tom can jump. Tom can run.

Tom can run and jump.

2. The dog can roll over. The dog can bark.

The dog can roll over and bark.

Add.

56	81	36	15
+ 3	+ 8	+ 3	+ 4
59	89	39	19

25	46	81	12
+ 2	+ 2	+ 7	+ 6
27	48	88	18

School Day Skills • Grade 1   243

Page 243

Answer Key

Page 244

Name _____ Spring • Week 7, Day 1

Add the blocks. Write the sum. The first one is done for you.

1. ▦ + ▦ = 61
2. ▦ + ▦ = 61
3. ▦ + ▦ = 42
4. ▦ + ▦ = 93

Divide each picture into equal **halves**. Color the pictures.

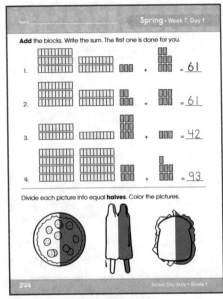

244   School Day Skills • Grade 1

Page 244

Page 245

Name _____ Spring • Week 7, Day 1

| back | call | king | pick | key | cake |

1. Write the words beginning with **c** that makes the **k** sound.

call   cake

2. Write the words beginning with **k** that makes the **k** sound.

king   key

3. Write the words ending with **ck** that makes the **k** sound.

back   pick

Have you ever seen a falling star? Falling stars are not really stars. They are small pieces of rock. As falling stars fall, they get hot and burn. They look big because they give off so much light. That is why they are so bright in the night sky. Did you know that **meteor** is another name for a falling star?

Circle the correct answer.

A falling star is really a star.   Yes   (No)

Falling stars are pieces of rock.   (Yes)   No

Falling stars burn as they fall.   (Yes)   No

School Day Skills • Grade 1   245

Page 245

Page 246

Name _____ Spring • Week 7, Day 2

Combine each pair of sentences into one sentence using the word **and**. The first one is done for you.

1. Mom plays with me. Mom reads with me.

Mom plays and reads with me.

2. Tara is tall. Tara is smart.

Tara is tall and smart.

Look at each word in **bold**. Circle the **prefix**. Write the root word on the line.

1. The (pre)view of the movie was funny.   view
2. We always drink (non)fat milk.   fat
3. I have (out)grown my new shoes already.   grown
4. You must have (mis)placed the papers.   placed

246   School Day Skills • Grade 1

Page 246

Page 247

Name _____ Spring • Week 7, Day 2

Write the numbers shown by the blocks. **Add** to find the sum.

1. 44 + 9 = 53
2. 83 + 7 = 90
3. 27 + 4 = 31

Connect the dots to draw one shape with four sides and one shape with three sides.

Shapes will vary.

School Day Skills • Grade 1   247

Page 247

Page 248

Name _____ Spring • Week 7, Day 3

Write an invitation for a party to celebrate your birthday. The party should last for three hours.

You are invited!

Where: _____

Date: Answers will vary.

Time It Begins: _____

Time It Ends: _____

Write **>** or **<** in the circle to show which number in each pair is **greater**. Make sure the "open mouth" points to the larger number.

11 (<) 100   18 (<) 48

52 (>) 25   77 (>) 27

248   School Day Skills • Grade 1

Page 248

Page 249

Name _____ Spring • Week 7, Day 3

When the sum of the **ones** is more than 10, **regroup** the **tens**. Look at the examples. Trace the numbers.

Step 1: Add the ones.   **Step 2:** Regroup the tens.   **Step 3:** Add the tens.

tens	ones
1	4
+ 8	
	12

tens	ones
1	4
+ 8	
2	2

tens	ones
1	6
+ 7	
2	3

tens	ones
3	8
+ 3	
4	1

tens	ones
2	4
+ 7	
3	1

| rain | day | sail | way | wait | say |

1. Write the **ai** words that make the **long a** sound.

rain   sail   wait

2. Write the **ay** words that make the **long a** sound.

day   way   say

School Day Skills • Grade 1   249

Page 249

Answer Key

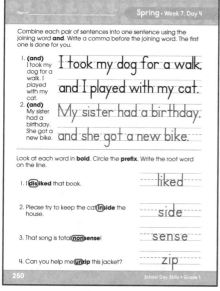

Page 250

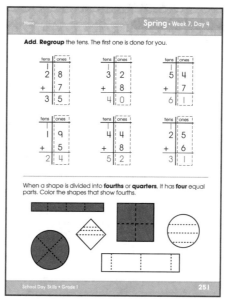

Page 251

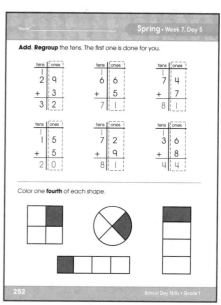

Page 252

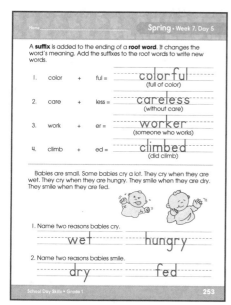

Page 253

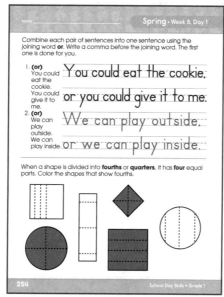

Page 254

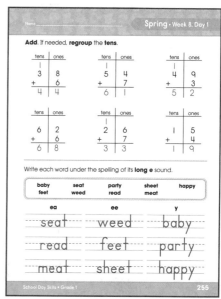

Page 255

Page 256

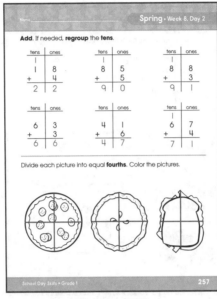

Page 257

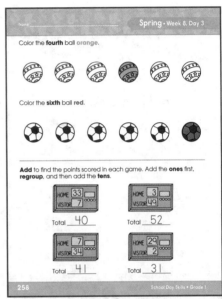

Page 258

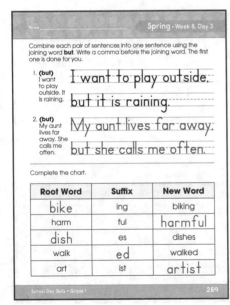

Page 259

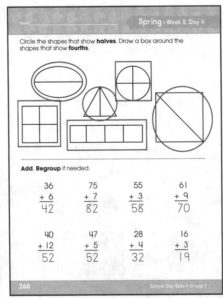

Page 260

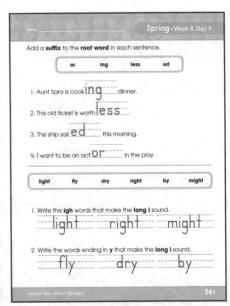

Page 261

Answer Key

Page 262

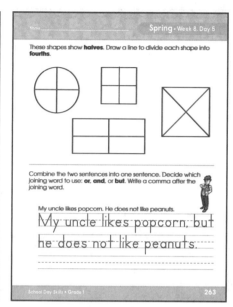

Page 263

Page 264

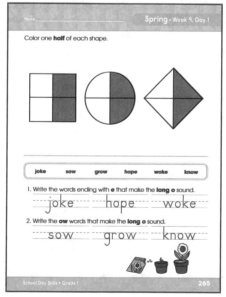

Page 265

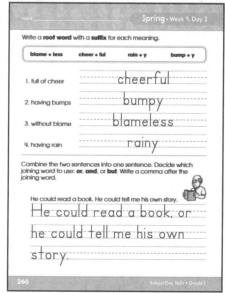

Page 266

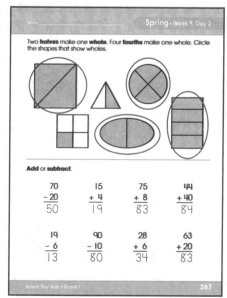

Page 267

Answer Key

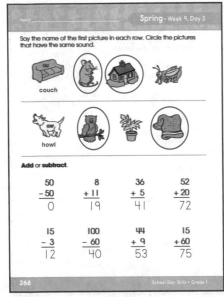

Page 268

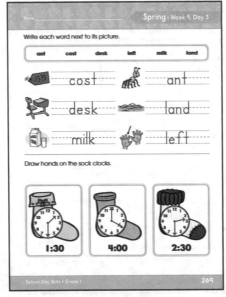

Page 269

Page 270

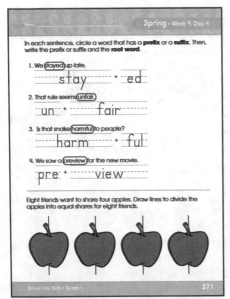

Page 271

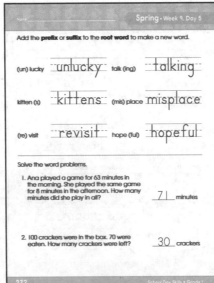

Page 272

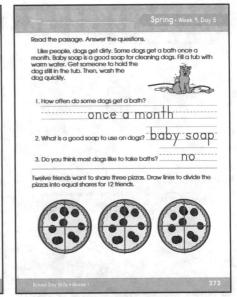

Page 273